THE FABRIC OF PLACE

THE FABRIC OF PLACE

ALLIES AND MORRISON
Edited by Bob Allies and Diane Haigh

Artifice
books on architecture

CONTENTS

The material included within the book takes three different forms:

ESSAYS relating to specific aspects of the work.

CASE STUDIES describing individual projects.

OBSERVATIONS highlighting particular issues.

CASE STUDIES

OBSERVATIONS

Introduction

This is not so much a book about the work of Allies and Morrison as a record of why and how that work came about. It draws together the various theories, precedents and influences that have provoked our work, and provides an explanation of why for us they are significant. It explores how existing settlements – villages, towns and cities – function, and why, sometimes, they don't. And it suggests how new buildings and new masterplans can help support their further evolution.

The book combines case studies of individual projects, essays relating to specific aspects of the work, and observations concerning the history of urbanism and the tools of contemporary urban practice. The case studies are intended to provide brief, but comprehensive, accounts of the evolution and rationale of each of the projects. The essays offer an opportunity to discuss at greater length some of the wider issues that the projects have had to consider, in particular those arising from the intensification of urban scale and density. And the observations illustrate more concisely, and more informally, some of the principles and processes that underlie the work.

The book is not intended as a textbook or primer, but rather as a series of reflections drawn from our direct experience of working with different cities, towns and villages. In this respect our concern has always been with the reality of what things are, with the need to understand how places work, and with what we, as designers, can do to support them. And underlying our approach are a series of implicit values informing and shaping the decisions that we make. The aim of this book is to make these implicit values explicit.

Cultivating the city

Bob Allies

To cultivate, according to the Oxford English Dictionary, is to "take something that exists, promote its growth, tend it, look after it, but also develop and refine it".

Of course there are circumstances where nothing exists, where new places, even entirely new communities, have to be built from scratch. But in most situations this is not the case. Sites that require the attention of an architect or an urban designer are nearly always situated within, or on the edge of, an existing settlement, a city, a town or a village.

And because of this, all such projects have to address the same fundamental questions. What should be the relationship between what is being proposed and what is already there? How should the new relate to the old? At its most straightforward this might be interpreted as an issue of context, of how as a designer one might best respond to the inherited history and topography of a site, or engage most effectively with the physical – and the social – fabric that surrounds it. But the significance of the pre-existing resides in more than just the specific context of the project.

The significance of the pre-existing

Settlements are the product of a myriad of forces, some complementary, some contradictory. Each has its own unique form and structure, a pattern that has evolved – often over centuries – through a combination of controlled intervention and pragmatic opportunism. However compromised, or unsatisfactory, or incomplete the resulting settlements might be, they still fulfil the same role. Cities, towns and villages accommodate – and articulate – the relationships between us, their citizens: how we live, how we work, how we interact. However diverse we might consider ourselves to be as a populace, the places in which we live are what we share. They are, if you like, what we have in common. Our settlements define us as much as we define them. And for this reason the existing structures that have given them their shape and the relationships that underpin them need to be treated as a critical component of any urban project.

In our projects we have always attributed significance to what is already there – to the site and to its context – and therefore to the nature of the relationship between the new and the old. We believe, for reasons that are social and economic as much as architectural or cultural, that buildings and masterplans should always be designed to respond closely to the context in which they are set, that they should reinforce, or in certain circumstances perhaps, reinterpret, the urban structure of which they form a part.

Allies and Morrison studios, Southwark with Farnham Place on the right, Bankside on the left, and the Shard in the background.

For us this seemed, until recently, to be essentially an urban issue. It was to do with how settlements work, and what settlements mean. But considered today in the context of contemporary concerns regarding sustainability it may also be regarded as an ethical issue.

For if we are to minimise our consumption of energy and materials it is not enough just to be efficient in the way we utilise new resources. We also have to explore every possible means of extending the life and the potential of those that are already in place. Cities, towns and villages are exactly such a resource. New buildings inserted in existing settlements and new masterplans intended to reshape them therefore have an obligation not just to work well in their own right. They also have to support the wellbeing and the longevity of the wider urban area of which they form a part.

The city as continuum

Human settlements—cities, towns and villages—are, arguably, among the most enduring of man's artefacts. Yes, sometimes they die: harbours silt up, mineral reserves are exhausted, industries decline, cultures wane. Settlements lose their reason for existence and their populations choose, or are forced, to abandon them. But in most cases they persist, continuously adapting in response to the changes in role or use that are imposed upon them. And as part of this process their physical fabric also evolves. Only in a city like Venice, where the dynamic of change has been artificially arrested, does it remain constant, a fixed record of a particular sequence of architectural, cultural and political development.

But this apparent resilience does not mean that settlements are invulnerable. No matter how obdurate they might seem to be, cities, towns, and villages are in many respects remarkably fragile, and interventions that are damaging to their fabric, new insertions that disrupt rather than strengthen their continuity, can easily cause damage, damage that in many cases may prove irreparable.

This is why we believe that every urban proposition has to be considered as part of a larger whole. At the same time as satisfying its own internal goals it should also be capable of supporting and contributing to the development of those parts of the city, or town, or village that lie outside its site. Without such an approach, settlements, whether large or small, rapidly dissolve into little more than an accumulation of discrete projects, sharing nothing between them, and unable to support the continuum of the wider urban fabric.

It is an approach which, at a detailed level, may sometimes influence the appearance of buildings. But its real importance lies not in its effect on how buildings look but on how buildings work. It suggests how buildings might best be assimilated into their immediate context. And it makes clear the role they might play as catalysts shaping and stimulating the future evolution of the city that surrounds them.

To attribute significance to the wider site in this way might be regarded as a sort of modesty, a willingness to subordinate one's own project to the generality of the context. In fact what it signifies is a far greater ambition, an awareness that each and every project has the potential to exert a positive influence across a far wider area than its own site, helping, say, to generate improvements in the quality of the adjacent public realm, increase opportunities for social and economic interaction and exchange, or reinforce identity and meaning.

Accommodating change

So, in giving new status to the pre-existing one is not arguing against change. Cities need the stimulus of change in order to flourish as much as they need the benefits of continuity in order to survive.

Sometimes this stimulus comes from a public authority, sometimes from a private initiative. Sometimes it comes from planners, sometimes from politicians. But in a city like London, which experienced rapid growth in the nineteenth century but is now attempting to resist outward expansion in favour of regeneration from within, it is just as likely to come from another, more impromptu source. Time and time again in London new generations of city dwellers, recognising the innate assets of a previously neglected area – the quality of its building stock, the convenience of its location, its relatively low land or rental values – have moved in and, through an investment in social as much as economic capital, have changed the area's status and given it new life. The history of post-war London is a catalogue of such unplanned and informal interventions: Chelsea, Pimlico, Notting Hill, Covent Garden, Islington, Wapping, Stoke Newington, Clerkenwell, Spitalfields, Brixton, Bankside, Shoreditch, Bermondsey, Hackney Wick, Old Street, have all been recolonised in this way.

There are those who are very wary of this phenomenon, arguing that its real effect is to displace the original inhabitants of these areas and destroy long-term social structures. But seen in the wider context of the evolution of the city as a whole, surely this capacity to reinvent and revitalise itself from within has to be regarded as one of its most exciting and extraordinary aspects?

In cultivating the city one is therefore always, necessarily, looking for ways to improve it, to make it more effective and more attractive as a background to our lives, to adjust it in response to changing needs and expectations.

Cities, towns and villages need to evolve. Indeed sometimes, notwithstanding the protestations of those protective of the status quo, they need to be allowed to evolve. Patterns of use mutate, construction and infrastructure technologies develop, land and property values fluctuate. At the same time, new opportunities arise and new obligations unfold. If we are to support our settlements in this process what is important is that we, as architects and urban designers, concern ourselves not just with the new elements that we are introducing but with the existing matrix into which they are being inserted. To cultivate the city is to add and to improve, but also to understand and to nurture.

London viewed from the Shard with Bankside, one of London's most rapidly changing areas, in the foreground.

Aerial view of King's Cross, 2004.

King's Cross Central

London

King's Cross Central is one of Europe's largest urban regeneration projects. The 24 hectare site is bordered by the new Eurostar line from France and bisected by the Regent's Canal. Its masterplan sets out a framework for the incremental development of a diverse mix of uses, embedded in one of the UK's most significant industrial heritage sites.

Today, the task that faces London – like many other post-industrial cities – is not one of expansion but of reclamation, of taking back into the city areas that have until now been allocated primarily to infrastructure – transport, industry, energy production, waste handling, docks – but which are no longer required for that purpose. And because of their central location, these areas also provide an opportunity to introduce new development often at a much higher density, a prerequisite for creating a more sustainable urban environment.

In Europe in the nineteenth century, it was the reclamation of the redundant defensive infrastructure of medieval walls and battlements that gave cities similar opportunities for renewal, for the creation of elegant boulevard rings – Nuremberg, Vienna – and, in many cases, the locus for a new generation of civic buildings.

In responding today to the challenge of reclaiming areas of redundant land, there are two approaches which might be taken. The first is to treat the prospective development as something completely new, a discrete urban proposition unrelated to its surroundings. The second is to understand it as part of a physical and historical continuum, a natural extension of the existing city. This is the approach we have taken.

St Pancras station – now renamed St Pancras International – forms the London terminus of the Eurostar service. Immediately to the east is a second station,

King's Cross. When seen on plan, the two stations, both built in the middle of the nineteenth century, seem to be on the verge of colliding with each other as they compete for position on the edge of the city. Between and to the north of the two stations lies an area of former railway land, land which became redundant in the latter part of the twentieth century and declined into dereliction and disuse.

The opportunity to redevelop this land at King's Cross came, as it did in Stratford City, as a by-product of the construction of the Channel Tunnel Rail Link: the land associated with the engineering project was given to the developers of the railway as a means of subsidising construction costs. Indeed, at King's Cross, the northern edge of the masterplan is defined by the line of the new railway as it emerges from St Pancras station.

The two Victorian stations are both significant pieces of architecture, but the entire site is of unique importance as a piece of industrial archaeology. The Regent's Canal which crosses the site from west to east was built between 1812 and 1820, and, because of the resulting reserves of water, the site became the location, soon afterwards, for the construction of one of the first gasworks in London: the four listed late nineteenth-century gasholders are being dismantled and re-erected as part of the project. A contemporary plan shows the gasholders, and also describes the configuration of the railway lines as they arrive at the two stations. As well as bringing in passengers

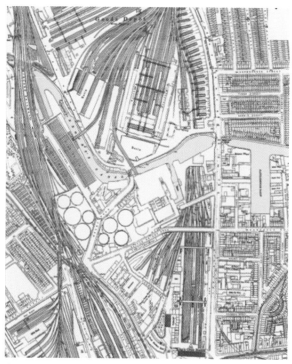

Ordnance Survey Map, King's Cross, 1894.

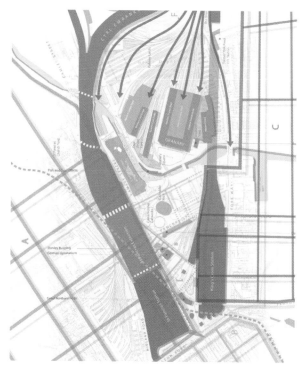

Plan diagram showing the relationship of the stations to the adjacent urban grids and the location of the historic goods yard and gasworks buildings.

in substantial numbers, the railways also delivered huge volumes of goods. So the organisation of the site evolved in direct response to the wider needs of the city, to the requirement to ensure the timely delivery of food, or beer, or bricks, into its heart.

One of the most remarkable configurations of historic buildings at King's Cross is that formed by the Granary and Transit Sheds. Fed by railway lines coming into the site from the north, the latter was designed with sheds on either side of the platforms so that horses and carts, could, in their turn, collect or deliver goods: trains entering from one direction, carts entering from the other. And in front of the building on the south side was a canal basin from which boats could enter underneath the building and receive deliveries from the trains as well. It was, effectively, the world's first intermodal freight interchange. In spite of its significance, it is a building that has always been curiously invisible to the public because, unless you happened to work there, it remained entirely inaccessible. One of the great opportunities of the King's Cross project

is that it has allowed buildings such as these to be opened up to the public for the first time.

At the outset of the project we looked for ways of describing the nature of the site, ways of understanding how the city works around it, where there were shops, where there was activity at street level. What was clear was that the site effectively formed a kind of void within the city, negating any relationship between it and its hinterland. At the same time, the site's extraordinary history, the way it had evolved, the pressures that had shaped it, were enormously important to us in generating the form and nature of the masterplan.

Just as the two passenger stations seem to have jostled for their positions on the Euston Road, so they adjusted themselves to the alignments of the pre-existing urban grids of which they were required to form a part: the Camden grid to the west for St Pancras, and the Islington grid to the east for King's Cross. In contrast to the passenger lines which draw closer and closer together as they approach the two stations, the freight lines effectively do the

Granary Building and Transit Sheds, King's Cross, watercolours;
Lewis Cubitt (1851). Boats can move from Granary Basin (left),
under tunnel, to arrive between train platforms (right).

The Fish and Coal Buildings on the north side of the canal with one
of the Victorian gasholders in the foreground.

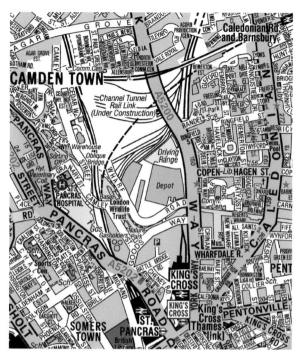

A-Z Map of London, existing.

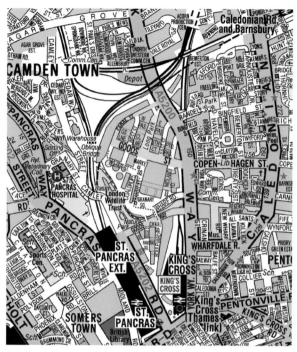

A-Z Map of London as proposed by the masterplan.

King's Cross Central: existing urban fabric.

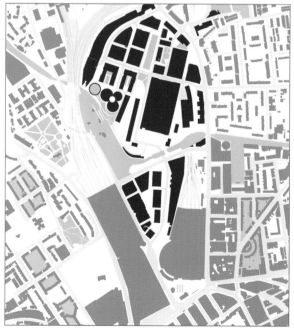

King's Cross Central: proposed urban fabric.

reverse, fanning out to take up more space when they finally arrive at the site. These functional geometries have left a strong imprint on the site, both in terms of the disposition of the buildings and in the manipulation of the ground. The masterplan grows out of these underlying patterns. Rather than impose a new geometric language onto the site, we wanted to explore how its history and topography might provoke unexpected formal and spatial relationships that would in turn give rise to a sequence of places that were unique, that were unlike anything that might be found elsewhere.

A single drawing produced early in the evolution of the King's Cross project sums up the intentions of the design. To the south of the site, between the two stations, is the first main public space. From here, two routes then lead north towards the canal. There is a concentration of density at the southern end of the site where the majority of the office accommodation – and the tallest buildings – will be located. As you move north and across the canal, the space opens up in front of the Granary, providing a setting for the main group of historic buildings which are being restored. Beyond this lies a further area of buildings with a combination of office, residential and hotel use. The shapes laid out in this image are not the buildings, but their disposition is intended to indicate something about the nature of the public spaces, the number and intensity of the cross routes, and the scale of the sub-division of the individual blocks. This is not the pattern which has to be built, nor is it a template for everything that must follow. It is the starting point for a process that will, of necessity, take many years to carry out.

In developing the project as masterplanners, Allies and Morrison and Demetri Porphyrios were able to benefit from the involvement of several other architects who were invited to undertake individual studies for a number of the sites. This provided a mechanism for testing the masterplan but also made it easier for everybody involved – client, planners, and the local community – to occupy, or inhabit, the plan at this early point in its gestation. What was important at this stage was to determine the nature and character of the spaces that would be created within

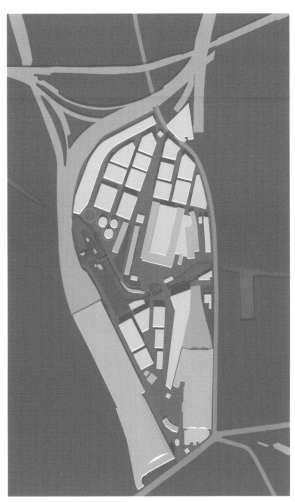

Early concept drawing.

Two floorplans illustrating anticipated concentrations of ground floor activity in yellow, orange and red in daylight (left) and at night (right).

Computer model of illustrative masterplan with schematic
renderings of individual buildings.

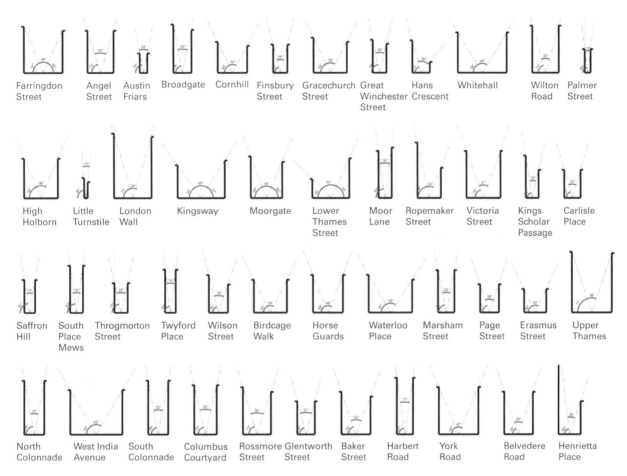

Farringdon Street · Angel Street · Austin Friars · Broadgate · Cornhill · Finsbury Street · Gracechurch Street · Great Winchester Street · Hans Crescent · Whitehall · Wilton Road · Palmer Street

High Holborn · Little Turnstile · London Wall · Kingsway · Moorgate · Lower Thames Street · Moor Lane · Ropemaker Street · Victoria Street · Kings Scholar Passage · Carlisle Place

Saffron Hill · South Place Mews · Throgmorton Street · Twyford Place · Wilson Street · Birdcage Walk · Horse Guards · Waterloo Place · Marsham Street · Page Street · Erasmus Street · Upper Thames

North Colonnade · West India Avenue · South Colonnade · Columbus Courtyard · Rossmore Street · Glentworth Street · Baker Street · Harbert Road · York Road · Belvedere Road · Henrietta Place

Comparative cross-sections through familiar London streets, prepared to explain and illustrate the urban scale proposed by the masterplan.

development zones and plot boundaries · maximum height limits · building lines define the edge of public realm · minimum elevation height defines the enclosure of space · setback-daylight cones encourage good daylight to buildings · illustrative built-out scheme

Sequence of diagrams showing how design guidelines and development specifications are intended to control building form.

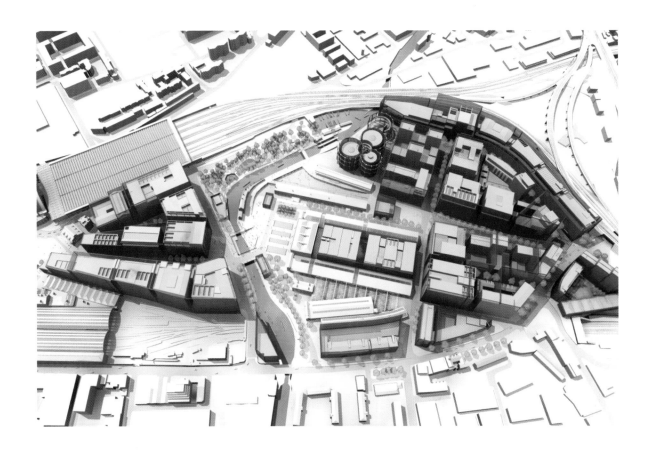

The translucent blue veil
superimposed on the computer
model of the illustrative
masterplan provided a means
of explaining the relationship
between the buildings as
illustrated and the maximum
permitted building envelope.

the masterplan in order to be able to define as clearly as possible the sorts of obligations that individual buildings would have to meet as and when they were brought forward. We wanted to ensure that the architects working on each of the buildings would have a clear understanding of the way in which their building had to address the various spaces of which it would form a part. This is one of the fundamental tasks of a masterplan, to provide each building with a sort of surrogate context, a virtual setting within which it can be designed, and against which it can be judged.

What also concerned us at King's Cross was how the new development might be drawn back naturally into the city that surrounds it, and avoid feeling like a separate precinct with its own discrete identity. We didn't want to emphasise where it starts and stops. Gateways, so beloved of planners, are to us anathema. What we were interested in was the way in which the masterplan might allow the development to operate simply as part of the matrix of the city. This is how to make it a better place, but also the way that the benefits of new investment might best be drawn out into a much wider area.

One of the key challenges of King's Cross was the development of a masterplan that would contain enough detail to give certainty of execution for the planning authority whilst allowing sufficient flexibility for the developer to evolve the scheme over a twenty year period of implementation, a length of time that would inevitably include some periods of recession.

The first issue was around the type and nature of the planning application. The site is a conservation area containing many important listed buildings. A detailed planning application though would have been far too unwieldy over a twenty year period. Constant revisions (and possible challenges) would have made the whole process risky, costly and unworkable. A simple outline application, however, would not have given sufficient certainty of outcome to the London Borough of Camden, the local planning authority or potential investors in the early stages of the project's implementation. The solution was a plan that proposed a chassis of streets, retained buildings and development parcels. Within this framework each development parcel had a degree of flexibility regarding uses, building heights, and floorspace quantum.

The framework was then tested through a series of design studies to ensure, block by block, that in its various permutations it would produce a piece of city that met the aspirations of the developer, the local authority and other stakeholders. This was then translated into a series of guidelines informing the stage of detailed design. Importantly these were not design codes which often prove over-prescriptive and stultifying, but they did provide the basis for the developer's procurement of individual buildings and have been used by them to control and monitor detailed designs as they come forward.

This was not a quick process, but it did allow a thorough investigation of the site, its context and a range of complex issues concerning the long term constitution and eventual management of the site. The developer was committed to long term ownership and therefore the management of the site. This meant that they had an absolute commitment to design quality. In many ways the operation and management of the estate constructed through the masterplan is as significant as the design itself. Key decisions not to seek very tall commercial buildings were driven as much by the developer's understanding of the market as by planning constraints imposed by strategic viewing corridors.

But the best test of the masterplan has been the experience of its implementation. The development had to weather the storm of the financial crisis of 2008. King's Cross Central was one of the very few projects that continued to build through this difficult period and is now indeed ahead of the programme envisaged when the planning consents were granted. The masterplan was not a blueprint, it was a framework that was flexible enough to frame the architecture of individual buildings and spaces.

This flexibility has allowed the client to respond to changing circumstances and adapt to opportunities presented by investors such as the University of the Arts and the Aga Khan Foundation. At the same time momentum has been established and the incorporation of the site's historic heritage has created a place with a strong enough identity to attract international companies such as Google and BNP Paribas.

And already King's Cross is a functioning and open piece of city.

The Granary, King's Cross Central, now home to the University of the Arts, London.

Palazzi del Campidoglio, drawing; Jean-Gilles Berizzi (1554–1560).

Building on the past:
the evolution of the Campidoglio

Palazzi del Campidoglio, etching; Giuseppe Vasi (1747–1761).

Michelangelo's Campidoglio is a unique architectural set-piece. Three buildings frame a carefully delineated urban space at whose centre stands the bronze, equestrian statue of Marcus Aurelius. It is a space that for Rome has huge historical and political significance: it is the *"omphalos"*, the navel, of the city.

But what is really compelling about the Campidoglio is the comparison between the form of the completed project and the pre-existing condition of the site.

For as the drawing on the left reveals – a sketch carried out when Michelangelo's project was under construction – the building that forms the centrepiece of the Campidoglio was built around a medieval core. What Michelangelo did was to provide this earlier structure with a contemporary facade, adding a new staircase and fountain at its base. The building to the right he also adapted and re-faced, retaining the form, but not the architecture, of the colonnaded front. He then added a further, symmetrical building in the equivalent position on the other side of the space. Finally, he adjusted the position of Marcus Aurelius allowing him to assume a primary role in the geometric and spatial organisation of the site, on axis with the grand flight of stairs that connects the site back to the city.

Michelangelo built both literally, and metaphorically, on the history and topography of the city. The result was an urban setting that must, at the time, have seemed at once entirely new, and entirely the same.

Three tales of the city

Paul Appleton

The historical sense involves a perception, not only of the pastness of the past, but of its presence.

TS Eliot, "Tradition and the Individual Talent", 1919.

Winchester, Hereford and Salisbury are all medieval cathedral cities, the pattern of building that we recognise today having been established largely between the eleventh and the fifteenth centuries. But while at first sight this common heritage seems to hold the key to their particular and precious character, their origins and history could hardly be more different.

Winchester was a Roman town, which after 400AD was almost completely abandoned under the threat of Nordic invasion. However, the pattern of the Saxon city that superseded it when the population returned some four hundred years later is aligned almost exactly with that of its Roman forebear. It is bounded by the Roman wall and defined by the lines of the Roman streets. And its high street extends from the place where the Romans first crossed the River Itchen from the east up to the location of the West Gate.

Hereford is a Saxon town. Its medieval streets follow the pattern of the original Saxon lanes, themselves defined by the coincidence of trading routes with the location of a defensive stronghold against the Welsh. The footprint of the city grew in the twelfth century but still remained within the area defined by the river and the city wall. The geometry of the modern city of Hereford therefore is the direct legacy of the Saxon settlement, its informal and irregular pattern entirely unlike the simple order and hierarchy we find in a Roman town.

Salisbury was a medieval 'new town', conceived and built between about 1217 and 1226 by Bishop Richard Poore who, responding to rivalry between the Church and the Army in the hilltop Old Sarum, chose to move his cathedral to an entirely new site on the plain. Situated at the confluence of five rivers and yet on land firm enough eventually to support England's tallest spire, Poore's new town was conceived as an ideal city plan, a gridded 'chequer' layout that survives almost entirely unchanged and is still legible today.

On arriving in an unfamiliar place one's natural instinct is to look for clues about its past. In historic cities, the relationship between the present and the past can seem almost palpable, the result of a process of continuous building and rebuilding in which nothing is allowed to stand still. In a good city certain things are permanent and immutable – topographic features, streets, spaces, views – while others, individual buildings, are more transient, ephemeral products of their particular age. Yet in the course of the nineteenth and twentieth centuries some cities appeared to lose this capacity to combine permanence and change so that this natural relationship between

Speed's map of Winchester
(1610).

Cole and Roper's map of Hereford
(1806).

William Naish's map of Salisbury
(1751).

Winchester   Hereford   Salisbury

the present and the past, this sense of continuity, was undermined. Subsequent chapters in their story have tended to be written instead more simplistically either in the language of preservation or of decay: areas of historic fabric are protected and conserved while others just a stone's throw away are neglected and marginalised. And it was areas such as these in Winchester, Hereford and Salisbury that began to be seen, towards the end of the last century, as potential cornerstones for the regeneration of the cities as a whole.

What is important now is that such stand-alone regeneration should not reinforce the earlier corrosive trend, the polarisation between development (of the new) and conservation (of the old). Instead, can we recognise and extend the enduring parts of our cities, acknowledging the present as a future past? This requires an understanding both of their 'physiology' (that which cities all have in common) but also their history (that which makes them unique).

Topography: the effects of water
A pivotal role in the siting and layout of each of our three cathedral cities was played by their topography. In each city, the rivers – together with their associated flood plain – have both defined its success and, in some areas, precipitated its decline.

In Salisbury such an area is the enormous surface car park whose name, the Maltings, reflects the nature of the Victorian industry that preceded it on the site. It is, and was, an area prone to flooding. The equivalent in Hereford is the now-vacated livestock market, severed from the city centre by an inner ring-road: also an area prone to flooding. In Winchester, it is the north-east quarter of the city, neglected as long ago as the eighteenth century and, again, an area prone to flooding. In each case the story is the same: nineteenth-century industrial use followed by incomplete twentieth-century road works; in all three cities, ring road projects planned in the 1960s and 1970s and facilitated by the presence of low value land, were abandoned because of the opposition of wealthy and influential householders in other parts of town.

A hierarchy of streets
What our three cities also share is a discernible weighting in the relative significance of the streets, something which is still quite legible and which is instinctively understood. Though each pattern is different, a product of the complex history of each individual city, there are certain characteristics that they have in common.

Each city has a recognisable commercial centre. Winchester's High Street (a Roman street dating from as early as 74AD), Hereford's High Town (where Owen Tudor was beheaded in 1461) and Salisbury's Market Place (in continuous use as a market since 1227) may share few historical or physical similarities but they each still represent the hearts of their cities: the places which people identify as their centre. Originally important arteries of trade, they have today become more symbolic than practical but continue to exert a tangible influence on the value and density of retail accommodation today.

The role of every other street within the city is defined by its relationship to this centre. Winchester's secondary streets run perpendicular to the High Street, providing important routes to the city walls and a legacy of the Roman plan; Hereford's Saxon lanes and Salisbury's still intact chequer-pattern of thirteenth century streets are both bisected by crossing trading routes. Like the map of veins and arteries in a body the hierarchy of streets is seldom described, even by those who know these cities well, yet is a pattern which, once detailed, is easily recognised and which seems to help explain a diversity, which is enjoyed instinctively by those who use it.

Continuity and individuality

In a medieval city, most of the buildings are subordinate to the streets they form. This is as it should be. The general jostling for space is only rarely disturbed, and only by buildings of significance, by ecclesiastical and civic structures which merit singular architectural attention. Today there needs to be a very good reason for new buildings to disturb this underlying order: it is their relative significance that should define their prominence and character.

Like a musical stave, Winchester's streets have provided a structure on which the notes and phrases of its two thousand years have been set. Individual buildings have never dislodged the underlying order, but have reinforced it, assisted by the fact that the size of individual buildings has been naturally limited by ownership boundaries. The natural ambition of the architect (and the damage that could be done by mediocre buildings) was largely limited – until the last century – by the scale of individual medieval plots. Buildings endure far less than streets and, whatever their quality, have a more limited effect on the character of a city. While it is true that poor buildings will always diminish a place, it is not always true that good buildings alone will save it.

In each of our three cities the regular, fine grain of medieval plots fronting onto streets still survives. It matters less to the character of the city which particular period these come from (there isn't a single remaining house in Winchester older than 1250, even though the plots are far older) than that they are – with a few exceptions – less assertive individually than as a whole. In Winchester therefore, the 'style' of any new buildings that we might propose is less significant than their relationship with the pattern of the city.

How can we repair the damage now?

When we attempt today to re-establish continuity, to create a bridge between the past and the future, one of the major challenges we face is the greater scale of the sites now being considered. This presents a philosophical dilemma; whether to represent or to subdue the pattern of contemporary ownership within the design.

Our approach is to work from the city towards the building. Firstly, new streets should adapt to their place in the city's hierarchy which is itself determined by value, position and topography. Within each street those things that affect its rhythm and

Winchester   Hereford   Salisbury

composition are then quite easy to identify: the width of a shop-front, a structural grid, a typical residential unit. All these encourage divisions which are familiar across these cities.

One way of responding therefore is to represent in new buildings the complexity of occupation rather than ownership. The return to the traditional model of retail and residential, of houses above shops, clearly helps. However, their ownership structure imposes a responsibility which no previous model had to confront: housing is independently owned and yet permanent (it is developed and then sold); retail is corporately owned and yet temporary (it is held by institutional investors and then rented). These places will be inherently difficult to re-assemble as large single sites and so, in order to retain value and therefore resist decay, must be readily divisible into discrete plots.

A supporting role

It is extremely unlikely, in a historic context, that any new intervention, however significant, will replace the commercial or formal centre of the city. It may bring more or larger shops; it may bring higher or denser housing. To be successful, however, it must take account of its relationship to the rest of the town. In all three cathedral cities – Winchester, Hereford and Salisbury – public recognition of the need for regeneration has been balanced by a natural anxiety about its possible negative effect on the existing centres.

We would argue that the new additions to a town will rarely justify major spaces or buildings to compete with those which have arisen naturally out of the history of a place. In contrast, our inclination is deliberately to put more rather than less pressure on these existing spaces, to rekindle their former liveliness. Winchester's Broadway, Hereford's High Town and Salisbury's Market Place had each, in the past, accommodated parading troops, jubilee celebrations and even political riots yet, for quite different reasons, each has become less vibrant.

If the historic centre itself can be improved, this will be to the benefit of any new development while, in return, new activity can breathe life into existing spaces. This virtuous cycle starts with an acknowledgment of the primacy of the high street, whatever name that takes, and is played out in a natural extension of the street pattern, perpetuating that often-delicate 'balance' around the centre which is a test of continuity and is clearly visible in the plan of a city.

The fallacy of scale

If the plan is the instrument we rely on most to understand the evolution of a settlement and promote its regeneration, what tools should we be using to address the vexed issue of height in the historic city? Cross-sections on their own tend to be misleading, perhaps unsurprisingly: one wouldn't expect to recognise the whole person through slices of a medical scan. While remaining resiliently recognisable over time, every single piece of a city like Winchester has grown, doubled, often trebled in height since the early middle ages. To attempt to limit height now by the application of rules is likely to prove self-defeating, while the simple equation of scale with character is a fallacy.

If towns and cities are to remain vibrant, it is likely that they will continue to grow. In certain areas this will quite rightly be prohibited by the value placed on the historic fabric; but what this means is that the pressure on sites deemed appropriate for development is even greater. A prescribed maximum height, such as that envisaged by the pre-existing planning guidelines for Winchester Silver Hill, will often have the unintended consequence of uniformity as it encourages building right up to that permitted limit. Nor is appropriate scale simply defined by the relation of height to street width. The widest streets in our cities are often the dullest – the pragmatic products of road engineering – while other narrow, tall alleys are captivating.

So while new buildings must emphasise, frame and enhance significant views, protect the intrinsic character of the historic centre and create an appropriate balance in the composition of the whole city, the effect of taller buildings in cities like Winchester, Hereford and Salisbury – whose heritage is of international significance – requires serious analysis to counter the simplifying (and stultifying) rule that no building must exceed a height defined by the present city.

A future past

We are looking for a way of understanding the city which will allow us to make proposals intensely particular to each very different place. This does not imply making buildings that mimic the existing or exactly match its scale, but it does imply appreciating and respecting both. It is not a simple prescription to match pre-existing patterns, in often quite chaotic parts of town, but does require an acknowledgement of the special status of the historic centre. The test is not whether we change these historic cities – that is inevitable – but whether this change will be able to be regarded, in the future, as part of a continuous process, as part of the future's past.

Winchester

Hereford

Salisbury

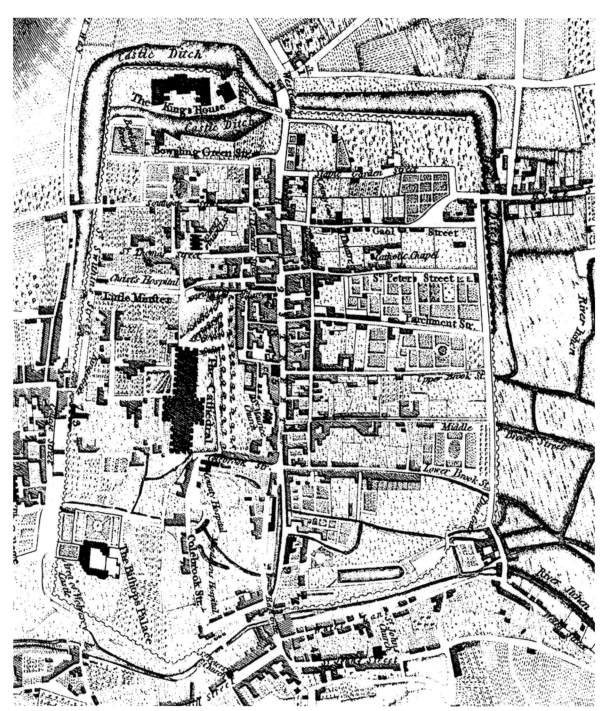

Godson's map of Winchester, 1750.

Silver Hill

Winchester

The introduction of new shops and apartments on the site of a redundant bus depot in the heart of Winchester's city centre provides an opportunity to repair its damaged fabric and reinforce its historic structure.

Any new addition to a city must absorb and support those essential characteristics which make it particular. In Winchester we tried to pin down those particular, enduring qualities and to apply them to the redevelopment of a whole quarter of the city: Silver Hill.

The first thing we observed was a remarkable continuity of plan over two thousand years.

One can easily miss this; modern maps are very matter-of-fact in their presentation. The first thing we did, before even a drawing, was to make a relief model of the city. This model only showed building, or absence of building, and water. This is like holding a candle under a page written in invisible ink; out of the ordnance survey map emerges a pattern which we found could be traced back through every available historic map; everywhere that was, except around our site, where the pattern seemed broken.

What we had recorded in this simple model were the three things which had endured, though individual buildings came and went: the hierarchy of streets; the pattern of fabric; the effects of topography. We chose to formalise these in a set of three further diagrams of the city and it was this that underpinned almost every subsequent decision.

Streets

Each street, it seemed, had adapted to its own place in a hierarchy which was affected by value, position and topography. Most significantly the formal value of each street was defined by its subordinate relationship with the High Street.

Remarkably, Winchester's streets, more or less, follow the plan of the Roman city of *Venta Belgarum*. However, the Saxon re-occupation did not simply settle upon its gridded pattern without discrimination. There is a discernible weighting of streets in the modern city which is quite particular to Winchester but which is fairly easily understood.

The east–west, Roman Decumanus Maximus is part of the road from London to Exeter and has retained its primacy, as a route, as a trading centre and as the focus for civic and public buildings. Secondary streets run north–south, from the high street to the perimeter of the city, its north and south walls. These streets are important arteries, routes around which trades developed. The tertiary streets (the 'back streets') tend to run east–west, behind the high street. They are informal and discontinuous; they may find the lines of underlying Roman streets but not all of them. As a consequence, they have a more static character.

This hierarchy of streets is not one which the average Wintonian would describe; it is uncovered through drawing plans and building models. Yet it is a pattern which, once seen, seems to help to explain a diversity which is enjoyed instinctively.

Winchester: existing urban fabric.

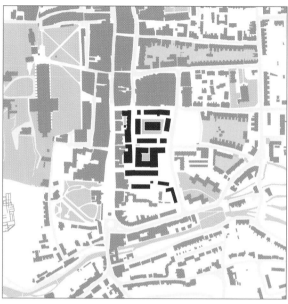

Winchester: proposed urban fabric.

The one part of the city where this pattern had been completely disrupted was Silver Hill. The pre-existing street pattern had been obliterated by the inaptly named Friarsgate (there was neither a friary nor a gate here), an inner ring-road which severed a series of secondary streets. Any proposals which we came to make would seek to repair this damage, to subvert the formal influence of this road. They should, we believed, reinforce the pre-existing hierarchy.

Sometimes this meant making the case against over-generous new spaces: Winchester is a city of streets not squares. In fact, the more pressure that the proposals

The East Prospect of Winchester, Samuel and Nathaniel Buck, 1736.

Winchester in 2003.

could bring to the extraordinary existing Broadway (the lower high street), the better this space would be. A fine farmers' market, for years housed pragmatically in a car park, will return to a Broadway reinforced, not dissipated, by new streets.

Fabric

This street pattern is supported by a loosely structured organisation of buildings; the built fabric of the city. The remarkable resilience of a city like Winchester to the erosion of its character is partly explained by the limitations of individual ownerships defined, largely, by Saxon plots. Buildings on these plots have been rebuilt, again and again; the oldest single house in Winchester is little more than seven hundred years old and much of the building within the town centre dates from the eighteenth and nineteenth centuries. Yet it is undeniably a medieval city.

Each period has produced its own architecture; limited by the size of a single plot (or at most two or three), no single building, however eccentric or undistinguished, disturbed the integrity of its street. The only exceptions to this were ecclesiastical and civic buildings, which deserved status and demanded quality.

Those areas of the city which lost this fine pattern of ownership were those which invited redevelopment. We needed to invent a way of making buildings which re-found the grain of the medieval city in amongst the new disciplines of shop fronts and residential units. Their orientation would prioritise primary over secondary over tertiary streets; groups of buildings would describe new streets which extended this pattern.

Within each new street modern shops, structural grids and residential units operate around dimensions which are already familiar throughout the city. This rhythm, though, is then allowed to respond to the particular conditions at every junction with an existing building, every view point from within and outside the city, every different internal discipline. Each new building treats its own neighbour, whether existing or proposed, as if the neighbour had been there first.

Before even contemplating the composition of buildings, therefore, one looked for a pattern which set them firmly in their context.

Topography

Winchester runs up a hill, away from the place where the Romans first crossed the River Itchen. Its division into four quarters effectively overlays the effect of water on the grid of the Roman city. The south-west hill had its fort, castle, palace and, much more recently, law courts. The equally protected high ground of the north-west still witnesses its trading, commercial and professional past in street names like Silver Street and Jewry Street. The south-east, the rich fertile plain, was set out from the ninth century as the ecclesiastical quarter: the cathedral; the bishop's palace; the college.

In contrast, the north-east quarter – low lying, often flooded – became the focus for leather working and fulling, around Tanner Street, Lower, Middle and Upper Brook Streets. It is this last quarter which subsequently declined; this was our site.

The topography explained the relatively low status of the site in the city; it was prone to flooding. It was precisely this low status which led it to be exploited by highways planners who constructed Friarsgate (and failed to complete their inner ring-road project in the face of resistance from the residents of more salubrious areas).

Yet it was water which might be the clue to its regeneration. Trained through the city by Saxon kings, who were otherwise denied access to the river by the church, a series of historic brooks recorded a lost street pattern, right across the site. Remarkably, the kings' brooks are still intact, under a surface of tarmac streets and yards; still flowing, still full of trout, like a living symbol of the continuing presence of the ancient city, just beneath the surface. So here was not only a record of streets but a clue to their extraordinary character (recorded in the remarkable nineteenth-century aquatint of Middle Brook Street).

Middle Brook Street, attributed to Samuel Prout RA, 1813.

A recognisable pattern.

The fabric of a city.

A process of evolution

There is no simple or mechanical process to magnetise new proposals around these markers of the resilient characteristics of a city like Winchester. They do, however, liberate new proposals from the obligation to stand alone. Instead, they are judged as participants in the whole city. While appropriately representing their content (or at least their initial content – occupation is even more transient than building!) each building is subordinate to its street and each street subordinate to the city.

The most obvious way that this affects the design of buildings is that the site ownership is suppressed rather than emphasised. So the edges of the site, where the development starts and finishes, are deliberately blurred. While the physical contribution to the streetscape will extend to the whole of Winchester's Broadway, we also hope that it will be difficult to detect, at the edge of our site, which buildings are new and which pre-existing; where exactly the junction is.

This is no cheap trick. It is a subjugation of the coarser instinct to mark out one's territory which, while that territory was a single plot, worked so well.

Similarly, while construction logic demands that each new 'plot', defined by four streets, is a single structure, such buildings would be larger than any in Winchester except the cathedral, the barracks or the crown court. Yet these new buildings will ultimately be occupied by a collection of individual home-owners and retailers. Perhaps their design could reasonably represent this finer grain.

So far we have made no mention of the visual language of buildings. That is because this is a secondary matter. It will always be the place where the most debate takes place, where the fiercest passions are aroused (Winchester was no exception) but the noisiest battles are often not the most significant.

It is not merely diffident to say that, once the structure of the new part of the city is right, the authorship of individual buildings is less critical. In our view, a successful language for these buildings will reinforce the underlying philosophy. It will exploit the tension in a relationship between medieval city and the demands of modern buildings. The architecture we have proposed for this new part of Winchester is therefore a description of the intersection of the permanent influences of the city (that which makes it particular to its place) with the influences of the brief (that makes it particular to its time). The studies of building types, which followed, illustrated this intersection. We believe it will be judged less for its style and more for its mix of order and informality; a balance which is perhaps the surest sign that this is part of a process of evolution of Winchester, rather than a compositional end in itself.

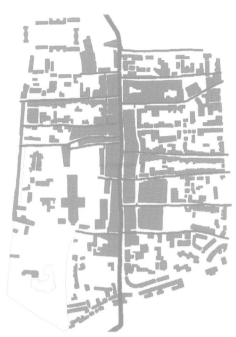

A hierarchy of streets.

Topography: the effect of water.

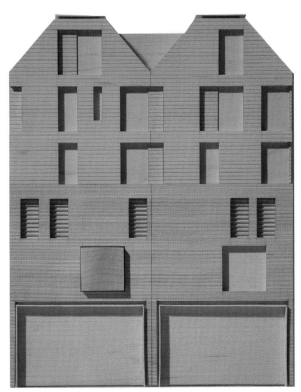

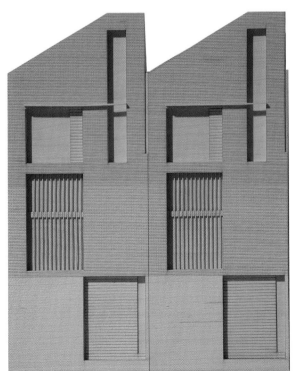

New buildings for an old city – a mix of order and informality.

Castle Street, etching; William Bartlett (1829).

The persistent street:

Castle Street, Salisbury

Castle Street, photograph (2008).

With the exception of the cathedral spire, almost everything in the view south down Salisbury's Castle Street, has changed since William Bartlett made his etching of 1829.

Yet the place remains instantly recognisable; while not one building has survived unchanged, the street persists – white vans and tarmac substituting oxen and compacted mud in the contemporary image.

On the whole, buildings are longer-lived than their occupants, their exteriors than their interiors, but buildings themselves are occupants of streets, which appear to turn on a much slower cycle. When streets persist, a city is resilient to the disturbances of ownership and occupation; it can wear the clothes of each new period confidently.

Bishop Richard Poore laid out Salisbury's streets in the early thirteenth century, beginning a story which is still being written and which shows no sign of ending.

When we imagine new streets, we are laying down an urban landscape which, though appearing to be defined by its buildings, is reasonably certain to outlive them.

Early photograph of Highbury Stadium showing its location in the
middle of an expanse of nineteenth-century terraced housing.

Highbury Square

London

By adapting two of the historic stands to residential use, retaining the area of the pitch as a shared garden and inserting additional housing around its perimeter, the former home of Arsenal Football Club has been preserved as a landmark within the city and integrated into the surrounding urban fabric.

Arsenal Football Club's decision to move to a new and larger stadium posed the question of what should happen to their former home at Highbury, a reservoir of memories for the Club and its supporters.

Embedded in the fabric of a typical London residential neighbourhood – its matrix of terraced houses interrupted only occasionally by post-war blocks of flats – the location of the former stadium was clearly a suitable site for new housing. But the stadium's 1930s Art Deco East Stand – one of the first purpose-built football stands in the world – was a protected building (Grade II listed) and therefore had to be preserved.

There is, of course, a long tradition of stadium buildings being preserved and adapted to accommodate new uses. One of Rome's greatest public spaces – the Piazza Navona – was created at the end of the fifteenth century from the remains of the first century Stadium of Domitian. Similarly, the Piazza dell'Anfiteatro in Lucca follows the footprint of a second century Roman amphitheatre, while the Roman stadium in Arles was, until its subsequent reclamation as an arena, entirely colonised for residential purposes. To a great extent, the Theatre of Marcellus in Rome still is.

The challenge of Highbury was how to acknowledge the cultural significance of this redundant building, this monument that had played such an important role in the identity of the local community for so long, while converting it to residential use.

Piazza dell'Anfiteatro, Lucca.

The Roman arena at Arles; the restored arena today (left), nineteenth-century engraving by LB Guibert (right).

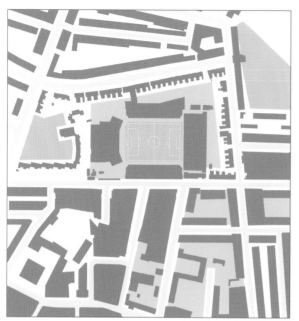

Highbury Square: urban fabric as existing.

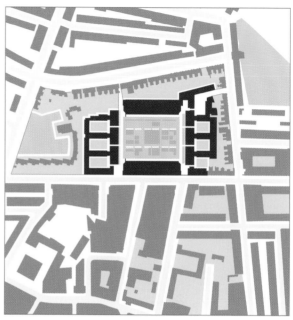

Highbury Square: urban fabric as proposed.

Early photograph of Highbury Stadium during a game.

There was also the question of scale. How could this large building retain its status within its setting while at the same time being assimilated into the much smaller scale of the local residential streets and squares?

In this respect the morphology of the stadium–a series of substantial, inward-looking structures grouped around the central space of the pitch–seemed to us to be a strength not a weakness. Rather than just keep the fabric of the one listed stand, we argued for the retention of the whole geometry and setting of the pitch. We therefore proposed retaining–and inserting new apartments into– not just the listed East Stand but also the slightly later, unlisted West Stand, while adding new, similarly scaled buildings to the north and south to complete the enclosure to, and preserve the memory of, the pitch.

The pitch itself became a new central garden–a contemporary London square–shared by all the residents. Hidden beneath its surface is a car park serving all the dwellings. The glass shafts that punctuate the landscape of the garden–designed by Christopher Bradley-Hole–

provide natural light and ventilation to this subterranean interior. And like a traditional London square, the new space also fulfils a wider role within the city, providing a new pedestrian route between Avenell Road and Highbury Hill.

So it is the pitch, now the new garden, which has once again become the focal point of the site, while a suitably dense urban residential community has been created around it. The scale of this development is substantial, and the character of the buildings – reflecting the scale of the existing stands – is open and expansive. Behind the buildings to the north and south of the pitch, a series of lower and more intimate courtyards adjoin the main garden, their facades dominated by the continuous balconies that front all the dwellings. Beyond these again, a variety of smaller buildings adjust the scale of the development to

the surrounding streets, in one case taking the form of a mews, in the other re-establishing the line of a terrace.

The design of the individual buildings varies according to their location within the scheme, responding in their scale, composition and rhythm to the character of their particular context. So, for example, while the buildings facing the open space of the garden are predominantly glazed, with strong horizontal proportions, the facades to the street are brick with a regular grid of openings in the masonry, and the elevations to the mews are more informal and finished in white insulated render. This inherently introduces a degree of variety into the development but, more importantly, it helps to blur the boundary between the new and the old, allowing the continuum of the city to reassert itself across the site.

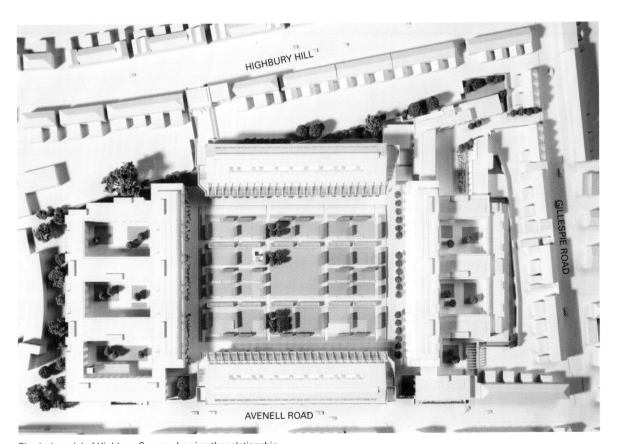

Physical model of Highbury Square showing the relationship between the central garden/pitch, the new courtyards to the north and south, and the matrix of existing streets surrounding the site.

Undercroft entrance into the courtyard.

Avenell Road frontage with listed stand (left) and new housing (right).

Overleaf: Highbury Square: the pitch has been transformed into a communal garden, with glazed shafts allowing light and air into the car park below.

Elevations to central garden.

New glazed facade to converted stand.

Residential mews.

On public, private and communal space

Bob Allies

One of the defining aspects of the structure of a settlement is the nature of, and the relationship between, its public and private space.

Private space might be described as space that is owned and maintained by a single individual, family or institution. Public space is space which is not only in the public domain but in public ownership. Space, that is, which is assigned to and maintained by the community, whether in the form of the parish, the town, the city or the state.

As citizens, we need both. We need spaces within our lives which are entirely under our control and which we can reserve entirely for our own use. But we also need spaces which we can share with our neighbours, spaces which we hold in common and for which we assume mutual responsibility.

Fundamentally, of course, what distinguishes public space from private space is the way in which it is owned. But in any consideration of towns and cities – and the ways in which we use them – what makes the distinction so significant is the manner in which these different types of space elicit different types of behaviour, each one offering us radically contrasting opportunities for privacy or security, interaction or exchange.

It might be argued that the most successful urban environments are those where the distinction between the public and the private is entirely unambiguous, where the dividing line between one and the other is completely clear. In a typical eighteenth or nineteenth, or early twentieth-century London street for example, the division between the private and the public, between the house and the street, is defined by the line between the pavement and the front garden, a divide sometimes made explicit by the evidence of a locked gate, but more commonly represented by the casual presence of an open one.

The value of this distinction is, not least, that it clearly defines the respective responsibilities of the two different land owners – the public and the private – to look after and maintain that which falls under their control. Spaces whose ownership is ambiguous, and for which neither party accepts responsibility, are exactly those which are likely to deteriorate and fail.

Nevertheless this simple polarity between what is public and what is private is not sufficient to describe the full spectrum of types of space that can be found, or created, within our towns and cities, nor the range of ways in which we can manage and operate them.

Within the last decade there has been a growing debate about the way the public domain has been subsumed by the private sector, with shopping centres and city

Typical London terrace.

Left: Burlington Arcade, Piccadilly, London.

Right: Central Market Hall, Budapest.

office quarters being cited as examples of this malaise. This 'privatisation of public space' has appeared not only to undermine the potential and vitality of our public life but, because of the manner in which it places control of the opportunities for civil engagement into private hands, has seemed to some observers even to threaten the resilience of our democracy itself.[1]

In fact the problem is not so much that existing public space is being withdrawn from the public domain and thereby privatised, as that what in new developments is being promised as additional public space is in fact being retained under private ownership and control. This is a real problem, and there is much to be said for the argument that urges more careful scrutiny of this process.

It is also important, however, to recognise that, historically, towns and cities have always included elements of publicly used private space, or, to reverse it, privately owned public space. The history of urbanism provides us with a number of precedents for more complex, and subtle, overlaps between public use and private ownership, most of which have generally proved helpful rather than hurtful to the evolution of our urban environment.

So in the example of the London street referred to earlier, the space of the front garden is inarguably in private ownership, but it is a space which at the same time acknowledges and allows an appropriate level of controlled public use. In a typical London street in other words, it is the front garden, or area, that both connects and separates the private world of the home from the public world of the street. It is semi-public, or semi-private, and its ambiguity in this respect is entirely beneficial. Conversely where, in London, the ground floors of houses have been converted to shops, the garden, or area, is removed and full public access is not just tolerated, but encouraged.

Cathedral precincts, shopping arcades, market buildings are all examples of private spaces which allow controlled public access, but which retain the capability to close themselves off at certain times of day and night. But there are also examples such as university campuses, churchyards, stations, airports or indeed rural rights of way, which although privately owned and controlled, nevertheless allow unrestricted access to the public at any time.

Conversely, while some public spaces – streets, squares, greens, commons – allow unrestricted public access, others, such as parks, limit access by members of the public to certain times of the day.

1. Perhaps the most well-known example is Anna Minton's *Ground Control: Fear and happiness in the twenty-first-century city*, Penguin 2012.

Left: Fitzroy Square, London. Shared garden enclosed by railings in centre of square.

Right: Maida Vale, London. Communal garden located at the rear of houses.

There are two points that are worth making here. The first is that to achieve an entirely appropriate level of public use, spaces do not have to be accessible to the public all of the time. And the second, is that the public use of space does not itself require public ownership: privately owned spaces can and do have a role to play in the framing of our urban life.

There is also, however, one further category of space which needs to be accorded its role within the structure of the city. This is communal space, space which is in the common ownership of a group of individuals – or families, or institutions – and which is maintained jointly by them.

In London, the most familiar and most famous example of this is the garden square, where the ownership of the central garden is shared between all those who own the houses on its perimeter. In fact the history of the London garden square is more complex. The first squares built in London in the seventeenth century were neither enclosed by railings nor planted, and it was not until the eighteenth century that residents, through private Acts of Parliament, sought permission both to enclose the central space and assume financial responsibility for its maintenance. Of these the first, in 1725, was St James Square, followed soon after by Lincoln's Inn Fields, 1734, Red Lion Square, 1737, Cavendish Square, 1737, Charterhouse Square, 1742, Golden Square, 1750, Berkeley Square, 1766, Grosvenor Square, 1774, and Hoxton Square, 1776.[2]

Today most of the squares in central London – whatever their legal ownership – are open to the public during the hours of daylight, while those outside the centre remain the preserve of those who live around them.

In a garden square it is the fronts of the houses that face the garden. In subsequent nineteenth-century London residential developments – in Notting Hill and Maida Vale for example – an alternative typology was developed in which communal garden spaces were drawn instead into the interiors of the urban blocks, allowing residents to move directly from their back gardens into the landscape which they shared.

In the twentieth century, driven more by an interest in the benefits of living communally (at least to a degree) than by a negative concern to protect against the outside world, a number of small-scale residential projects tested out a modern equivalent. The small terraces of family houses designed by Howell and Amis, in South Hill Park, London, 1956, and Neave Brown, in Winscombe Street, London, 1964, both sacrificed space at the back of the houses in order to gain larger areas

2. Longstaffe-Gowan, Todd, *The London Square*, London: Yale University Press, 2012, p. 55.

Gated housing estate,
Souillac, France.

of communal gardens. The careful manipulation of the distinction between the private and the public domain, the layering of public, semi-public, private and semi-private space was key to Brown's architectural proposition and constituted an explicit rejection of the ambiguous and indeterminate open space that he believed characterised other contemporary schemes.[3]

At a larger scale, the SPAN developments designed by Eric Lyons and Ivor Cunningham in the 1950s and 1960s in London and Cambridge were arranged around areas of shared green space jointly maintained by all the residents. Land that might have been included in private gardens was effectively reallocated to the common domain. The Span estates were never enclosed, or separated, remaining a privately owned part of the public realm. Since then however there has been a growing tendency to add just such a barrier around similar estates, a measure which has prompted widespread criticism, with the phrase "gated communities" invoked in condemnation.

In fact what makes the notion of a gated community so problematic is not the creation of communal space *per se*, but the manner in which the communal ownership is overlaid on the generic, physical structure of the conventional city. What really disturbs is the disruption caused to the continuity of the public domain, not the principle of communal spaces being separated from it. It is, in other words, the arbitrary withdrawal of a section of the highway, or street, or footpath from public use – the moment where the divide occurs – that seems so offensive.

In our understandable rejection of the gated community we should not however lose sight of the importance of 'communal space' as a legitimate and valuable component of the urban environment, particularly in those areas where – for reasons of sustainability – we are now electing to build at much higher densities than we have in the past.

For a family living in a flat, on an upper floor, in the middle of a city, the benefit of an immediately accessible secure area of communal space cannot be overstated. The knowledge that your children can play safely and mix with others without requiring direct supervision is enormously reassuring. Common ownership helps to encourage community cooperation. Mediating between the public and the private domain, communal space – space that is shared, space that is protected, space that is set apart – has an important part to play in the shaping of the twenty-first century city.

3. Swenarton, Mark, "Developing a new format for urban housing: Neave Brown and the design of Camden's Fleet Road estate", *The Journal of Architecture*, vol. 17 no. 6, December 2012, pp. 982–984.

Aerial view of Royal Festival Hall showing the building encircled by
upper level walkways following the expansion of the site in 1964,
with service road cutting the building off from the river front.

Royal Festival Hall, Southbank Centre
London

Like many post-war cultural centres, the Southbank Centre was originally designed and planned as a discrete institution standing apart from the rest of the city. Today, as part of a major refurbishment and renovation of its interior, the Royal Festival Hall has re-engaged with its surroundings to become a crucial part of the public life of the city.

The Royal Festival Hall, which opened on 1 May 1951, is the only physical legacy of the Festival of Britain, that optimistic celebration of the post-war revival of the nation's economic and cultural life. During the Festival the newly cleared South Bank site was populated with a series of temporary pavilions linked by intriguing routes and meticulously arranged public spaces. This gaiety lapped around the edges of the Royal Festival Hall and its architects reciprocated by extending the main foyer level out on to balconies and terraces facing the river.

The design of the concert hall followed a simple diagram. Within the external envelope, the auditorium was raised above a spacious public foyer–'the egg in a box'–with entrances and staircases on either side winding up to a succession of upper level foyers and culminating in roof terraces at the top. The clarity of its concept was essential to the speed with which the project was delivered: it was conceived, designed and constructed in a period of just thirty-two months.

The tight timeframe and budget constraints meant that the Royal Festival Hall could not be fully completed in 1951. In 1964 it was extended with a layer of new foyer space to the riverfront and an additional bay of back-of-house accommodation to the south. This was also the moment when the newly enlarged Southbank Centre, which now included the Queen Elizabeth Hall and the Hayward Gallery, was linked to Waterloo with high level walkways. These encircled the Royal Festival Hall and moved the primary

public entrances to the river frontage. The effect of this was to undermine the whole logic of the original organisational structure of the building. Recovering the circulation diagram by returning the main entrances to their original position was the first move necessary to allow the whole plan to make sense again.

In the original design, the public foyers were seen as generous flowing spaces that extended out on to the

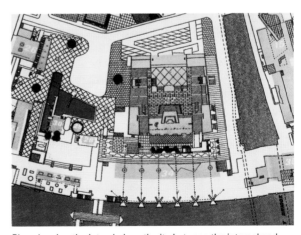

Plan showing the intended continuity between the internal and external terraces in the Royal Festival Hall, Architectural Review (August 1951).

River frontage, 1998, with the service road at the lower level and upper walkway above.

River frontage, 2008, with new restaurants under the terrace relating the building to the river.

surrounding terraces. This transparency had subsequently been blocked by shops and cafes that had colonised the building. Clearing them out to reopen these remarkable spaces has reversed this trend, and allowed performance events to return.

In the masterplan for the South Bank Centre that Rick Mather prepared as a precursor to our work, Mather proposed the insertion of a narrow building to the west of Royal Festival Hall immediately alongside the Hungerford railway viaduct. This new 'liner' building would serve the Royal Festival Hall at all levels and provide a line of commercial

units for the displaced shops and cafes. Similarly, the South Bank Centre offices were moved into the upper levels, which liberated spaces which they had previously occupied within the hall itself. Down at ground level it provided badly needed back-of-house facilities to serve the auditorium. These were accessed from the far side of the Hungerford Bridge, the arches providing additional storage, support space and loading bays.

The new liner building, completed in 2007, is one of the key urban design moves that has framed the setting of the Royal Festival Hall. It also defines the route for commuters

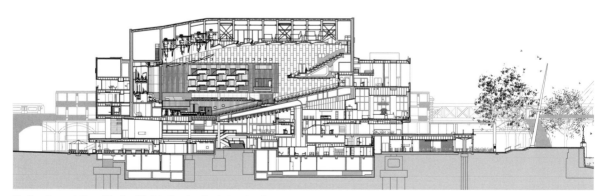

Section through Royal Festival Hall to the riverfront showing the new relationship to Belvedere Road (left) and the river promenade (right).

Upper level walkway in 1964.

Upper level walkway in 2008.

New promenade level restaurants with the upper level terrace above.

from Waterloo station who flood across the Hungerford pedestrian bridge every day. Sitting outside the footprint of the Grade I Listed Building, it establishes a commercial base for the South Bank Centre and generates revenue for the support of the Arts programme.

The moves that opened up the Royal Festival Hall internally, also spread out like ripples to re-establish the wider urban context. Through a broad series of stairs and ramps on the north terraces, the building reattached itself to the riverfront Queen's Walk where a line of cafes and the bookshop now thrive along the waterfront. Meanwhile at the upper terrace level, which is now linked to the ground by two major staircases marked by canopies, the foyers can be opened up

to the terraces as was always intended. On the Waterloo side a new square is created on Belvedere Road, which places the Royal Festival Hall in a more formal setting. The inclusion of a new restaurant and the 'Spirit Level' education centre has established a new presence for the building on this side.

The urban life of the Southbank Centre has been transformed by the scrupulous refocussing of the original design intentions of the Royal Festival Hall, the insertion of new restaurants and commercial spaces to repopulate the terraces and the provision of new opportunities for the Southbank Centre's open arts policy. Together they have allowed this piece of London to emerge again as a hugely popular public place.

Steel pavilions containing lifts connect the foyer to the river.

The new 'liner' building defines a new street alongside the Royal Festival Hall.

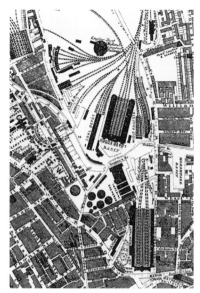
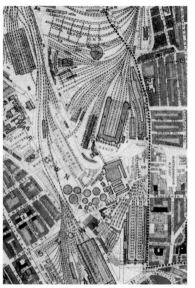

King's Cross Station and the Northern Goods Yard dominate the site.

Booth's property map of 1889 shows the diverse social and economic character of the site.

Aerial view of Regent Street overlaid across the site as scale and density comparison.

OBSERVATION   **Plans and their purposes**

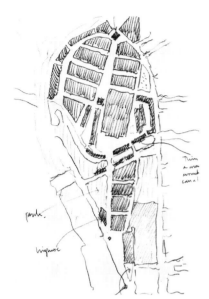 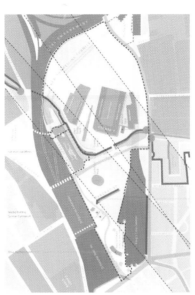 

Sketch scheme of a sequence of linear development zones (Porphyrios Associates).

Plan showing how viewing corridors towards St Paul's Cathedral constrain the development height.

Existing ground floor uses are centred upon King's Cross station.

During the preparation of a masterplan, drawings perform a myriad of functions. Drawings are used to understand and explain the site, for the tentative exploration of first ideas and the rigorous testing of developed ones. Drawings convey degrees of fixity and promise degrees of flexibility. Drawings describe options and set out alternatives. Drawings record constraints and define problems.

The drawings on the following pages – all site plans – represent a small sample of those prepared during the development of the King's Cross masterplan. They provide an account, and a record, of a process that began at the start of the masterplanning process and continues today as the project is implemented.

The sequence in which the drawings are shown follows the chronology of the project, starting with historic maps and diagrams analysing the character and constraints of the existing site followed by sketches exploring different ways of configuring the accommodation, drawings setting out the illustrative design, plans defining the parameters for the development and maps showing the new proposal in the context of the existing fabric.

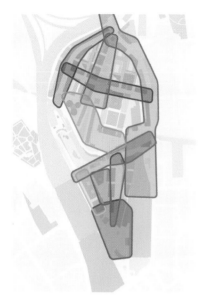

Overlapping zones, each with a different character.

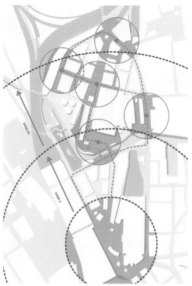

Pedestrian walking times across the site from the transport hub.

Late morning sunlight study of the illustrative masterplan.

Plan of the heritage structures and transport infrastructure as existing.

Diagram showing how existing buildings are embedded within the masterplan.

Late evening sunlight study of the illustrative masterplan.

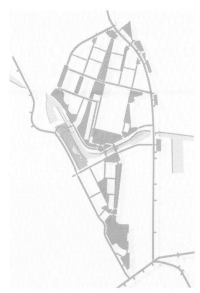

A network of proposed streets and public spaces.

Illustrative masterplan.

Illustrative masterplan embedded into the city.

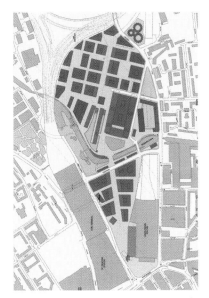

Sketch scheme of different uses distributed along a central spine and two new squares.

Physical model of a version of the illustrative masterplan.

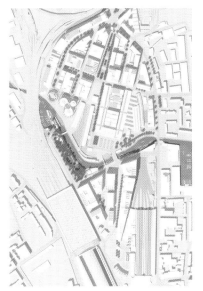

Illustrative masterplan showing an example of balanced development.

In common

Bob Allies

Human settlements take many forms. They vary in their size, from hamlet to village, village to town, town to city, city to metropolis, and they vary in their density not only between each other but within themselves. Just as cities invariably consist of a high density, urban core bounded by a low density suburban periphery so villages habitually take the form of a nucleated centre, which becomes more dispersed and fragmented as the built fabric of the village folds into the landscape that surrounds it.

Cities, towns and villages also vary in the manner in which they are configured and in the built typologies of which they are made. History, topography, use and governance all have an impact on the forms their buildings take and on the relationships that are established between them.

And, of course, settlements differ radically from one another in the quality of the physical environment they provide and, more particularly, in the consistency and coherence of the fabric of which they are composed. So while some towns and cities, or some areas of some towns and cities, achieve a pattern of built form and spatial enclosure that entirely transcends the quality of the individual pieces – the buildings, the streets – of which they are made up, others remain entirely inconsequential, no more than the sum of their various, disconnected parts.

The urban matrix

There have been occasions when the pattern of a town or a city has been drawn up by a single agent: a landowner, a public authority, a planner, an engineer. More typically, however, it is something that has evolved both gradually, over an extended period of time, and collaboratively, through the participation of multiple parties. Indeed even those settlements whose form was initially determined by a single, prescribed plan have still invariably required the involvement of many different individuals for their realisation.

What this evolutionary process relies on is an understanding that the fabric of a settlement should be treated not as a series of isolated buildings or disconnected projects, but as a single continuous matrix, a matrix to which all parties are able to contribute and, just as importantly, one to which they are also prepared to conform.

In our view, this matrix – this pattern of streets and spaces that structures our physical and social environment – is at its best when it is most contiguous. And, conversely, it is least satisfactory when it is most fragmented. What determines the quality of a settlement – more than the integrity of the individual buildings of which it is composed – is, in other words, the extent to which the resulting physical fabric comes

Canal-side street in Venice.

together to form a continuum. This is something that applies as much to the fabric of a town or a village – or indeed a suburb – as it does to that of a city.

When we attempt to characterise the nature of this fabric specifically in the context of a city, we conventionally describe it as "urban". Curiously, and frustratingly, there is no equivalent adjective that we can apply to these same characteristics when we encounter them in the context of a town or a village. It was this that led the archaeologist Jacquetta Hawkes, in 1951, to fall back on the phrase "rural urbanity" to characterise the towns and villages of the Cotswolds in her remarkable, and personal, history of Britain, *A Land*.[1]

The qualities that Jacquetta Hawkes so much admired in these towns and villages half a century ago – their physical containment, their underlying hierarchy, the continuity of their fabric – still seem compelling today. These are qualities that are at the heart of urbanism. What is also striking about these settlements is the way in which all – or at least the majority – of the constituent parts elect to respond to their location in a similar way, also a key characteristic of the urban. This phenomenon – very obvious in a medieval town or village where buildings are constructed from a similar palette of materials and stand closely side by side – is just as evident in the centres of nineteenth-century cities – Paris, Manchester, Budapest – where the discipline of the street controls and unifies the configuration of the urban fabric. But it is equally an observation that can be applied, say, to the buildings of a Norwegian fishing village where the houses are set apart from each other but share a common relationship to the fall of the land and the presence of the water. You can, in other words, find urbanity in a village as much as you can find it in New York. When assessing the urbanity of a human settlement it is the consistency of the response, not its nature, that is important.

In some ways it is this very quality that makes a city a city, or a town a town: in a town or in a city, everybody builds their own buildings, but they also contrive to build streets. Much more than just the accumulation of a series of individual initiatives they are the outcome of a shared endeavour. The result is what Aldo Rossi has described as a "collective artifact".[2]

It is because they are the product of such a consensus that places as diverse as Rome or Chicago, Valparaiso or Hebden Bridge, are acknowledged – from the perspective of the anthropologist as much as the urbanist – as some of man's most extraordinary achievements. And why, when towns and cities fail to secure such a consensus – when individuals act unilaterally, without any relationship to their neighbours – they seem, in contrast, so unrewarding.

1. Hawkes, J, *A Land*, The Cresset Press, 1951, p. 122.
2. Rossi, A, *The Architecture of the City*, Cambridge, MA: MIT Press, 1984, p. 113.

Terrace formed of individual buildings connected by party walls, at Knightsbridge, London.

The protocol of the handshake.

In most instances these relationships are governed by conventions, or regulations, a set of common protocols which all participants are prepared to follow. Of course we rely on such protocols in all forms of human inter-relationships. The handshake and the embrace are physical protocols that have evolved to facilitate greetings between strangers. It is exactly because they are conventions – because they are commonly accepted – that the level of intimacy they allow seems both acceptable and appropriate.

In a city street, what first controls and governs the relationship between two adjacent buildings is the presence of a party wall. The party wall imposes rules to which both buildings are required to conform. Paradoxically, just as much as these rules control the way the two buildings are conjoined so, at the same time, they liberate each building and allow it to assume its own form and identity. The same is true of a second crucial urban rule, the building line. While the building line, if adhered to, provides a way of ensuring consistency in the alignment of a succession of adjacent properties, and therefore a mechanism for controlling the relationship between building and street, it does not at all imply a limitation on the architecture of the individual buildings that contribute to it.

These relationships, and the mechanisms that control them, are important because they are what determines the city's form and character. But they are important too because they also allow the individual pieces of the city – the buildings – to evolve and change over time, in the secure knowledge that the overall context – the frame – is going to endure.

This is not to suggest that to create a successful city, town or village everything within it needs to be the same, but what it does mean, we think, is that the buildings which constitute it and the spaces which they enclose should form part of a continuum. Every piece should connect to every other piece.

In some places – in the sorts of places referred to above – these relationships are so well established that all buildings naturally conform to them and, in so doing, also reinforce them. In these cases the character and status of the individual building – its particular needs – are subordinated to the requirements of the whole. What this gives rise to is a singular, consistent morphology, a form or pattern which all the constituent parts support, and to which they all conform.

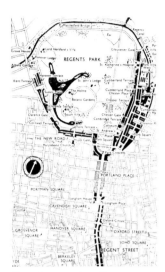

The urban set-piece: Regent Street and Regent's Park; John Nash, 1811.

Such a situation occurs most straightforwardly where the individual components of which the fabric is made up are most similar to each other, similar in terms of use, scale and the technology of their construction.

It was this situation that prevailed up to the end of the nineteenth century. But by the middle of the twentieth century, things became more complex. New technologies changed the way people built. New requirements affected the form that buildings took. And new notions of viability and efficiency encouraged the aggregation of larger development sites, whether by private developers or public agencies. At the same time a growing obsession with individual expression, with the idea that a building represents some form of personal statement by the architect or the client, encouraged the idea of standing out rather than fitting in. Innovation was prioritised over conformity, and the continuous fabric of the city was sacrificed to one composed of individual, disconnected pieces.

Of course, to a great extent, the composition of cities, towns and villages is indeed made up of just such individual pieces. Sometimes these pieces are single buildings; sometimes pairs or rows of houses; sometimes they are institutions; sometimes streets, or squares, or parks, or promenades; sometimes they are whole estates and sometimes entire neighbourhoods.

Each piece, inevitably and reasonably, expresses to a degree its individual identity. And there is, certainly, always a place within cities for urban set-pieces. In London, the early nineteenth-century plan for Regent Street and Regent's Park – conceived and implemented by the architect John Nash – survives as one such piece, notwithstanding the fact that Nash's original buildings in Regent Street were largely replaced in the early twentieth century, and that, like many large scale urban projects, its construction caused a rupture in the fabric of the surrounding city that, almost two hundred years later, is yet to be fully repaired.

But in terms of the role each of these pieces play in the making of a city, more important than what sets them apart is what they have in common. However significant to the identity of a town or city are its individual set pieces, what ultimately determines the quality, the character, and the consistency of its urban fabric is the level of consensus shared by the everyday buildings of which it is composed. This is the means by which the whole becomes greater than the sum of its parts. Indeed, it might be argued that great cities – or great parts of cities – are so, exactly because the majority of the buildings which constitute them respond to their context, or operate within their context, in an essentially similar way. In this respect what they have "in common" is of far greater significance than what sets them apart.

This is why finding an appropriate balance between the expression and identity of the individual piece and that of the wider urban order is an essential, if often neglected, aspect of the design of buildings and the conception of large urban projects.

For us, in the design of individual buildings it forces a judgement as to the status of the new structure relative to the context in which it is located. In the design of groups of buildings it raises the question of whether they should all conform to a single identity or be allowed to develop individual characters and identities in order to facilitate the integration of the project as a whole into its context. And in the development of a masterplan it means adopting and extending urban conventions that are consistent with the surrounding urban fabric so as to emphasise and reinforce continuity rather than exaggerate difference.

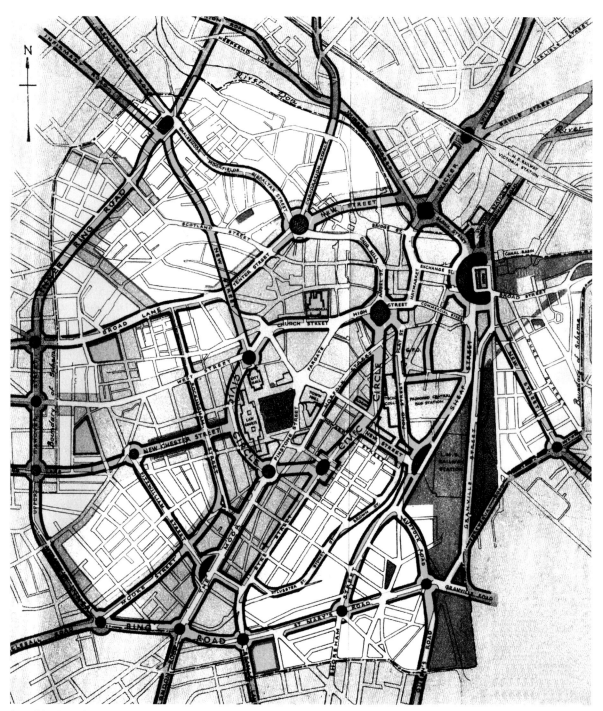

City of Sheffield Central Area Road and Zoning Plan 1945.

Heart of the City

Sheffield

Intended to reverse a decline in the use and status of Sheffield's city centre, this project re-established a strong urban structure in the heart of the city with a succession of buildings framing a sequence of both new and re-imagined public spaces.

Our involvement in Sheffield began in 1994 when we were appointed by the City to develop a masterplan to revitalise the city centre.

Essential to this process was a decision already taken by the council to demolish its own civic offices – a 1960s behemoth that contributed little to the city's public realm – and use this as an opportunity for a radical re-imagining of the character of the city centre that would also embrace Peace Gardens, Tudor Square, the Cultural Industries Quarter and Sheffield Hallam University, as well as establish a more direct pedestrian connection between the city centre and the station.

Central to all of these objectives was the need to overcome the barrier of Arundel Gate – a post-war dual carriageway created as part of the city's inner ring road – both by considering new ways in which it might be crossed and by encouraging future buildings to turn to face it rather than back on to it as was originally assumed.

Although not realised until after the Second World War, the idea of the ring road was first put forward by the City Engineer in the 1930s, one of a number of such ambitious plans prepared by British cities at that time in response to what was already expected to be an explosion in car ownership and usage. The Sheffield plan imagined an entirely new urban structure extending across the city centre to provide not just a new road infrastructure but a sequence of generous (if dull) civic buildings and spaces.

The first studies prepared for the city centre focussed on re-establishing a clearer urban matrix of buildings and spaces.

Town Hall and Peace Gardens from terrace of 2 St Paul's Place.

View of 1 St Paul's Place from Peace Gardens.

Norfolk Street looking north.

View from Peace Gardens.

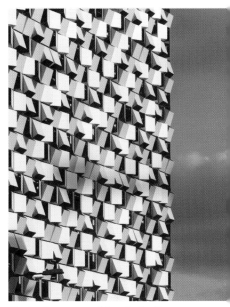

Charles Street car park facade detail.

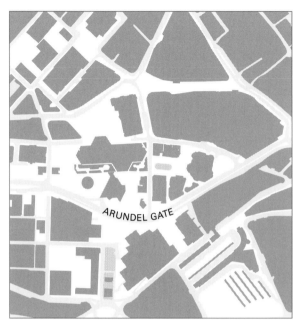

Heart of the City, Sheffield: urban fabric as existing.

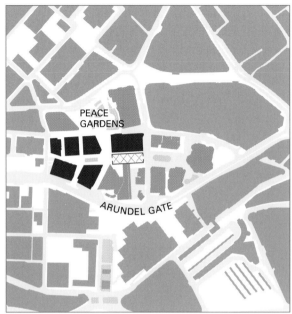

Heart of the City, Sheffield: urban fabric as proposed.

In practice, as in so many other British city centres, the intention of the new road network – whatever benefits to traffic movement it provided – did untold damage to the fabric of the city, creating scars that have yet to heal, more than fifty years later.

Our 1994 masterplan established a series of tasks which the subsequent redevelopment of the site was then required to fulfil. These included a stronger connection between the station and the city centre, increased accessibility across Arundel Gate, a public realm link between Tudor Square and Peace Gardens, the reinstatement of a clear urban structure with smaller, individual buildings on the site of the 1960s civic offices, and the re-invention of Peace Gardens as a major public space. These objectives were defined in such a way that they could be brought forward via a series of separate initiatives in a process that is still underway.

Our involvement continued in the detailed planning and design of one of these areas – St Paul's Place – immediately to the west of the already constructed Winter Garden (our original external public realm connection rendered as a dramatic internal space).

This more detailed masterplan replaced the civic offices with a pattern of urban blocks that re-established the former street pattern and facilitated movement across the site. The new buildings – a combination of office, residential and hotel use with shops, cafes and restaurants on the ground floor – were configured around a second new public space to the east of Peace Gardens, which was itself terminated with a new multi-storey car park, conceived as a significant civic building in its own right.

Opposite: Concept model showing the configuration of the new buildings.

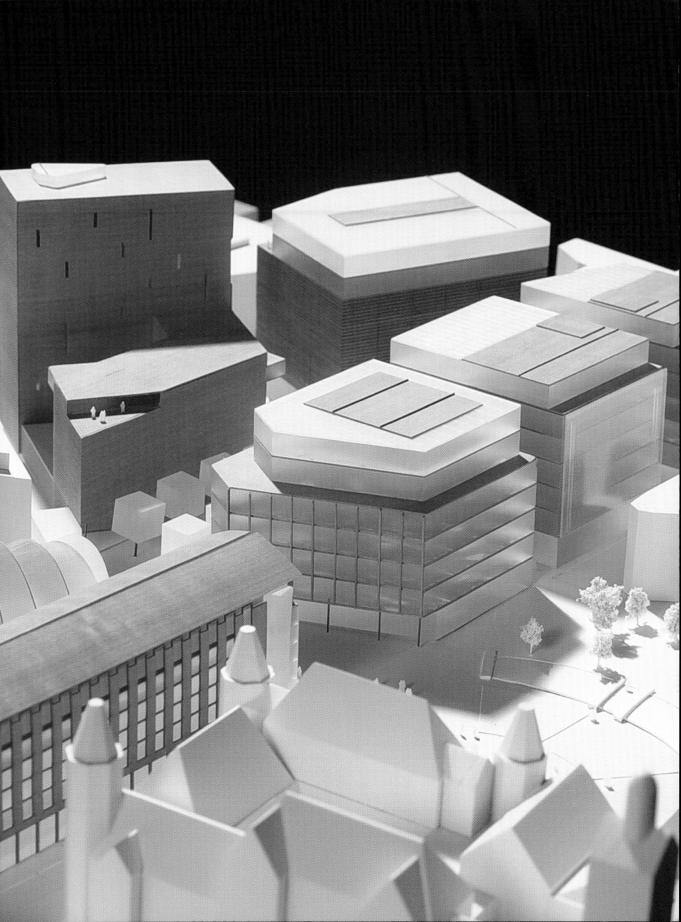

OBSERVATION   **How buildings participate:**
the urban facade

Allies and Morrison studios, Southwark Street, London.

The attitude to the city that is explained and explored in this book is as relevant to the practice of architecture as it is to the discipline of urbanism.

How individual buildings work within the city – how they support the urban hierarchy, sustain the building line, frame external space, respond to their neighbours, address the street – is critical to the coherence and continuity of the city. To build in the city, in any city, is to participate in an essentially cooperative process, and comes with obligations as well as opportunities. Of these, perhaps the most obvious is the need to reinforce the continuum of the street with buildings that are appropriate in terms of their scale, their uses, their rhythm. This does not mean 'fitting in' – and certainly not designing new buildings to resemble existing buildings – it means acknowledging the presence of established urban protocols and designing new buildings to accord with them.

These protocols are important both in the way they clarify physical relationships between buildings, but also the way they inform the interface between buildings and the passers-by. The photographs on the following pages illustrate a series of urban facades designed by the practice.

City Lit, Keeley Street, London.

South Place Hotel, London.

Bankside Two, Southwark Street, London.

6 Brindleyplace, Birmingham.

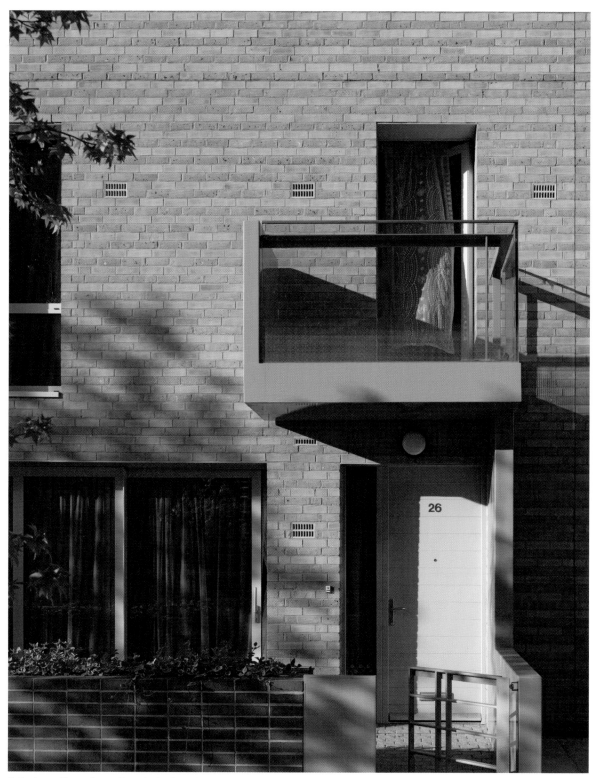

St Andrews, Devas Street, Bromley-by-Bow, London.

Highbury Square, Avenell Road, London.

Why we are where we are

Robert Maxwell and Bob Allies

The significance of the British contribution to the evolution of town and country planning in the twentieth century cannot be overstated. Yet what is also true is that in that same period there was hardly a town or a city in Britain that was not damaged – in many cases irreparably – by the planning and architectural orthodoxies that then prevailed. Ring roads, shopping centres, housing estates all eroded the continuity of the fabric of our towns and cities by failing to assimilate themselves into the pre-existing urban condition and leaving in their wake a residue of unresolved and unusable spaces. Repairing this damage has become an increasingly important aspect of contemporary urban practice.

One of the underlying causes of this phenomenon was an assumption prevalent during this period – among architects as much as planners – that the individual components of the city – roads, housing, shopping, offices, industry, culture – would be best addressed by separating them out and treating them as discrete problems each with their own solutions. So roads were designed with the single objective of facilitating traffic flow, a goal that was most easily achieved by isolating the highway from all other activities. Housing – whether high-rise or low-rise – was delivered in the form of individually designed estates, disconnected from the fabric of the town or city that surrounded them. Shopping was drawn away from the street and into enclosed malls, sometimes even being removed from the town centre entirely.

This latter possibility, that key town centre uses such as shopping – or indeed offices – might be extracted from urban centres and placed instead on their perimeter, only intensified the problems that these centres had to face. By drawing life and activity away from the centres, the euphemistically named "retail parks", "business parks" and "industrial parks", inevitably weakened the towns on whose perimeter they were located, diminishing their social vitality and undermining their commercial viability. A particular irony then that what made these out-of-town schemes so attractive to developers was their easy accessibility by car, an unintended consequence of the ring roads and bypasses introduced to relieve pressure on the centres from which this exodus was now occurring.

This erosion of the continuity of the fabric of town and city centres was only made worse by a concurrent tendency for the majority of new public buildings – theatres, hospitals, libraries, health centres, schools, museums – to be conceived as free-standing structures set apart from their immediate surroundings. In the first half of the century – in the pioneering years of early Modernism – this isolationist approach

Typical fragmentation caused by a post-war relief road, Godalming, Surrey.

might have seemed justified as a way of separating new buildings physically, and symbolically, from the discredited urban fabric within which they were situated. But the legacy of this approach as it played out over the rest of the century – and, indeed, as it still survives today (whether now for reasons of architectural hubris or merely as a means of simplifying funding or facilitating procurement) – has only led to further unnecessary fragmentation. How different to the manner in which the Victorians and Edwardians integrated their cultural and philanthropic buildings firmly into the fabric of their towns and cities.

What gave rise to this situation?

Two questions dominated urban planning in the first half of the twentieth century, both before the Second World War – when assumptions about the nature of the nineteenth-century city were being challenged – and after, when the opportunity to replace and rebuild urban centres resulted from the destruction caused by aerial bombing.

The first question was how the inherited problems of towns and cities, many of which had suffered from decades of rapid and uncontrolled expansion, might best be ameliorated. These problems were perceived primarily as overcrowded and sub-standard housing; inadequate and inequitably distributed open space; and the coincidence, and therefore conflict, between homes and industry.

The second was how best to accommodate the anticipated exponential growth in motor car ownership and usage.

In the 1920s and 1930s a new generation of architects and planners – Modernist in outlook and socially aware – attempted to confront both these issues, proposing new paradigms for the design and organisation of mass housing as well as suggesting radical ways in which our deficient city centres might be entirely reconsidered.

Reacting against the excessive density and enclosure of the traditional city, and influenced in part by the low rise models pioneered by Raymond Unwin and the English garden city movement, a group of European architects sought more rational solutions to the problems of housing. Rather than being clustered around tight courtyards, "*Zeilenbau*" houses were organised in parallel lines suitably orientated and spaced to maximise their access to sunlight, daylight and open space. At the CIAM Congress in Brussels in 1930, Walter Gropius went further, exploring through a series of diagrams how even greater efficiencies might be achieved using the *Zeilenbau* model if the blocks were to be spaced further apart and their height increased accordingly.[1]

1. Swenarton, M, *Building the New Jerusalem: Architecture, housing and politics 1900–1930*, 2008, pp. 70–71.

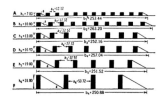

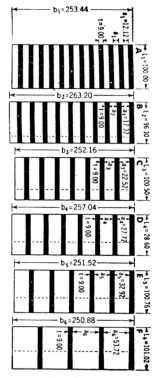

Analysis of relationship between building height and spacing. Walter Gropius, 1930.

Six years earlier, the architect and urbanist Le Corbusier had already published his manifesto "The City of Tomorrow" in which he set out his own, radical vision for the future of the city.

It was an extraordinarily ambitious, wide-ranging, and heart-felt document, part meditation on the history of urbanism and the nature of dwelling, part catalogue of the emerging technologies that he recognised were destined to shape the coming century, and part detailed physical proposal suggesting what form the city of the future might take, from the broad description of buildings and roads to the intimate detail of the home. Extending to over 50,000 words and including more than 200 plates – a torrent of photographs, sketches, cartoons, diagrams, graphs, drawings – it was by any standards a remarkable feat of publishing.

And because underpinning the book was Le Corbusier's belief that the city in its present form could not survive, that its inadequacies in the face of modern needs and requirements, and densities, would inevitably make it redundant, the book was also a call to arms: "The 'corridor-street' between its pavements, stifled between tall houses, must disappear", he proclaimed.[2] "The centres of our cities are in a state of mortal sickness, their boundaries are gnawed at as if by vermin.... Therefore my settled opinion, which is quite a dispassionate one, is that the centres of our great cities must be pulled down and rebuilt."[3]

In Le Corbusier's "City of Tomorrow", in contrast to the nineteenth-century city against which he was reacting, three new principles took centre stage: the zoning of uses, the generous provision of green space and the prioritisation of the car. And his assumption that the old city would be replaced by the new was one that was widely shared up until the early 1970s: it seemed inevitable and logical that the failing, existing fabric would in due course be entirely replaced, with a new spatial condition.

But while the polemics of these and other modernist architects in the first half of the twentieth century were enormously important in helping to shape the character of much post-war development, they were not alone in suggesting ways of improving the urban environment. Ideas for change were coming from all quarters, from politicians, engineers, public administrators, doctors, philanthropists.

The importance of increasing the amount of open space available to residents, for example, was recognised in England as early as 1925 with the imposition – in new developments – of a minimum standard for the provision of land dedicated to recreation of two hectares per 1,000 population. Already in the nineteenth century many local authorities in the UK had also introduced byelaws imposing minimum standards of separation between dwellings. Today, minimum distances between buildings of 18, or 20, or in some cases 25 metres are still required by many local authorities: a standard that was easy to achieve in the low density environment of the suburb or the new town has in other words become widely adopted as a measure to which all new development – even, incongruously, in the centre of cities – is expected to aspire. By forcing buildings apart however it effectively neuters our ability either to retain the intimate, enclosed character of our historic villages, towns and cities or to recreate equivalent intensity in modern developments.

One of the first determined attempts to resolve the conflict between different land uses is also to be found before the end of the Second World War in the ambitious and wide-ranging 1943 *County of London Plan* prepared by Abercrombie and Forshaw. Taking the area of Shoreditch as an example, the authors first analysed and mapped the complex, overlapping mix of uses that then existed on the site before setting out

2. Le Corbusier, "The City of Tomorrow", F Etchells trans., The Architectural Press, 1947, p. 134.
3. Le Corbusier, "The City of Tomorrow", p. 110.

a new vision showing how conflicting uses might be separated out, redistributed and reorganised in different parts of the borough. It was an approach that was adopted in most subsequent land use planning in Britain, at least until the end of the century.

Today, current thinking is beginning to move in the opposite direction, welcoming mixed use and opposing zoning, the latter finally being recognised as, in most circumstances, being contrary to the very urban qualities we are endeavouring to achieve. Indeed in our masterplans we try, wherever possible, to preserve flexibility in the range of permitted uses within development parcels as long as possible.

Today too, as we search for the most sustainable solutions to our urban problems – higher density living, the more efficient use of land, a greater engagement with our historic town centres – overly prescriptive regulatory systems controlling privacy, overlooking and the provision of open space – imposing suburban values in urban situations – are also beginning to seem anachronistic.

If the first question confronting planners and engineers in the middle of the last century was how to deal with the inherited problems of the nineteenth century city, the second was how best to respond to the anticipated growth in car usage in the twentieth century city. Although generally not implemented until the 50s and 60s, plans to introduce entirely new highways schemes within a number of English cities – Sheffield, Plymouth, Liverpool – were being developed long before the outbreak of the Second World War.[4] Laid out according to the latest highway engineering principles, with gently curving roads linked by generously dimensioned roundabouts in order to maintain higher speeds and increase traffic flow, these schemes required a level of site clearance and demolition that posed a real threat to the fabric of these cities long before the advent of war-time bombing. Similar proposals were also included in the County of London plan, with local ring roads, roundabouts, street widening, flyovers and underpasses just some of the measures identified as being necessary to achieve the required highway improvements.

By the end of the war, the Ministry of Transport itself published a circular which acknowledged the growing significance of the motor car and imposed four key, new criteria for the design of major roads in towns and cities. Through traffic, it proposed, should in future be completely separated from local traffic. Side connections onto through roads should be reduced to an absolute minimum. Subways and over-bridges should, wherever possible, be preferred to at grade crossings. And buildings facing onto major highways – buildings, in other words, with front doors onto the street – should be avoided altogether.[5]

The purpose of the Ministry of Transport proposals was to speed up the flow of traffic, reduce journey times and minimise the number of accidents, particularly involving pedestrians. Whether or not it succeeded in this, what it manifestly did was undermine the principles on which the traditional city had worked, making roads that were difficult to cross, creating urban contexts in which it was difficult to build and leaving public spaces which were impossible to use. In attempting to satisfy the needs of the car, all other aspects of how streets contribute to the functioning of the public realm were disregarded. Or more fairly perhaps, were never understood.

An extreme example of this disjunction between an urban plan designed to serve the car and an urban plan designed to serve the pedestrian appears some twenty years later in the 1963 *Buchanan Report*, a study commissioned by the government to explore the implications for urban areas of the next fifty years expansion in car usage.

4. For a comprehensive and illuminating account, see Alan Philip Lewis, "A History of Sheffield's Central Area Planning Schemes 1936–1952", unpub. PhD thesis, University of Sheffield, 2006.
5. Ministry of Transport, "Design and Layout of Roads in Built-up Areas", 1946.

Plan of Fitzrovia, London, prepared by Colin Buchanan as part of the
1963 report showing the scale of new roads required to accommodate
the anticipated increase in car ownership. Euston Road is at the top
of the drawing and Oxford Street at the bottom. Great Portland Street
and Tottenham Court Road form the western and eastern boundaries.

In order to carry out his study, Buchanan – who had qualified as both a highways engineer and a town and country planner – first had to assess how many private cars might be expected to be on the road fifty years hence, in 2013, and his projections in terms of numbers have proved to be remarkably accurate. Buchanan suggested a figure of thirty million; the actual figure is 28.7 million. So his assessment of the scale of the problem was substantially correct. His report then examined what scale of intervention would be required within our urban centres to cope with these sorts of numbers. This he did by considering four different types of context: a small town (Newbury), a large town (Leeds), a historic town (Norwich) and a large urban block in central London (in fact an area defined by Euston Road to the north, Oxford Street to the south, Great Portland Street to the west, and Tottenham Court Road to the east).

In each case Buchanan first carried out a careful analysis of the existing situation and then proposed a number of alternative scenarios each offering different degrees of benefit in terms of car usage: "minimum redevelopment", "partial redevelopment" and "complete redevelopment".

Viewed retrospectively, the level of change suggested under "complete development", is simply staggering. To be fair to Buchanan it was not something that even he thought would happen "for a generation at least". [6] Nevertheless his conclusion that "schemes on the lines we have explored are far from being unrealistic" does convey something of the contemporary mood and reflects the widespread conviction at the time amongst politicians and town clerks as much as engineers and planners that radical measures would have to be adopted if we were indeed going to cope with the rise and rise of the motor car. [7]

The negative impact on the physical character of our towns and cities caused by the unilateral requirements imposed by the Ministry of Transport at the end of the war and the prevailing assumptions about the prioritisation of the car cannot be over-emphasised. They changed the way in which our town and city centres were organised, determined to a great extent the layout, and therefore the urban character, of all the post-war English new towns, and they wrought extraordinary damage on the fabric of countless small historic towns up and down the country.

Today, fortunately, planning policy is generally directed not so much at accommodating the needs of the car as finding ways of assimilating it into the everyday life of the city. Improved public transport provision, better cycling arrangements, car clubs, parking fees, congestion charging have all played their part in liberating us from the need to replan completely our towns and cities. But in many locations the damage has already been done, and our task now is to explore ways in which we can repair the fabric and help these damaged areas to cohere again into real pieces of city.

The reason for revisiting this period of planning history is not just to set out the background to the tasks we face today. Nor is it to apportion blame for earlier failures: every planning policy and urban theory described above was the product of an intensely serious and rational attempt to solve the problems that contemporary towns and cities faced, whether these were problems inherited from the past or anticipated in the future. The real purpose is to remind ourselves that the fabric of our settlements remains just as vulnerable today to ill-informed interventions – whether well-intended or not – eroding the key urban qualities of continuity, coherence and community. And therefore that as we, in our turn, take responsibility for shaping this fabric in accordance with our new needs and objectives – social, environmental, political, financial, architectural – we should be alert to the consequences of the measures and approaches that we adopt.

6. Buchanan, C, *The Buchanan Report*, London: Penguin Books, 1963, p. 200.
7. Buchanan, *The Buchanan Report*, p. 200.

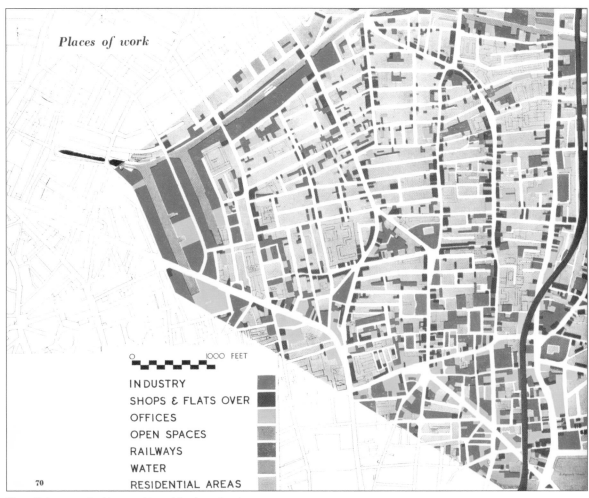

Places of work

INDUSTRY
SHOPS & FLATS OVER
OFFICES
OPEN SPACES
RAILWAYS
WATER
RESIDENTIAL AREAS

0   1000 FEET

70

Shoreditch: survey by Abercrombie and Forshaw showing
disposition of land uses, as they existed in 1944.

OBSERVATION   **Back to the future:**

between two ideals

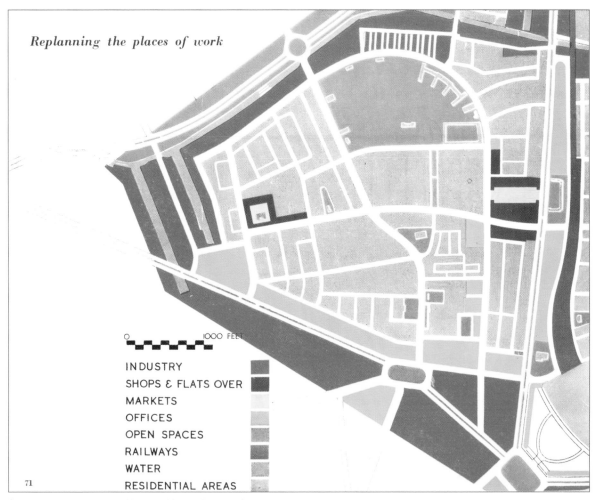

Replanning the places of work

O ■■■■■■■ IOOO FEET

INDUSTRY
SHOPS & FLATS OVER
MARKETS
OFFICES
OPEN SPACES
RAILWAYS
WATER
RESIDENTIAL AREAS

71

Shoreditch: proposition by Abercrombie and Forshaw for rationalising land uses and open space, allowing the separation of industrial uses from residential uses.

A reminder of how serious London's urban problems seemed in the first half of the twentieth century – and of the radical nature of the solutions developed in response – is provided by these two drawings. Taken from the *Greater London Plan* of 1944 – one of two remarkably ambitious plans prepared for the city by Abercrombie and Forshaw while the Second World War was still in progress – the drawings focus on the particular issue of the relationship between housing and industry. The first drawing shows the East End borough of Shoreditch as it was in the late 1930s – a jumble of small streets and lanes with a mixture of different land uses – and the second how it might be redeveloped in the future with new wide roads, generous public green space and separately zoned estates of industry and housing.

It is ironic that sixty years later, contemporary urban theory probably favours the former rather than the latter.

Aerial view of Coventry city centre showing the area enclosed by
the post-war ring road.

Friargate

Coventry

Anticipating ever-increasing levels of car ownership, the masterplan for the post-war reconstruction of Coventry removed cars from its centre and introduced a multi-level ring road at its perimeter. The problems of this plan have since become clear and overcoming its stranglehold is now an urgent issue for the future evolution of the city.

Following the devastation wrought by air raids on a single night in November 1940 the heart of Coventry's city centre was rebuilt according to designs prepared by Donald Gibson, the city's first official architect. The new Broadgate, ironically much of it car free, was opened in 1948. The introduction of the ring road into the fabric of the rebuilt city, which was begun in the late 1960s and completed in 1974, was intended to provide unrivalled access to the city centre. Its route was considered to be safely beyond the boundaries of the centre and the remains of the medieval ramparts and walls. It was a bold statement of permanence built in reinforced concrete, which symbolised the strength of the car industry and its importance to, and influence on the city, a physical embodiment of the resurgent confidence of post-war Coventry. The growth in the size and number of cars and the corresponding carriageway space needed was not fully anticipated, despite contemporary American experience.

Coventry had been one of the most complete medieval cities in the country, surrounded by substantial ramparts, wall and gates designed to defend its inhabitants and withstand a siege. Access and trading through the gates was regulated and limited. The construction of the modern ring road mimics this, but whilst it has increased the ability to enter in horseless carriages it has greatly reduced the ease of access by foot. Instead the ring road necklace acts as a tourniquet, unintentionally dividing the outer parts from the core.

Our involvement in Coventry began in 2008 when we were commissioned to explore again a masterplan for the area to the south of the city centre and the railway station that had been promoted for a number of years, but had stalled. Friargate, the *nom de plume* for our masterplan, includes Greyfriars Green at its northern end, a green swathe that funnels into the city centre like an old drovers route to the original Grey Friars gate.

Coventry is in need of a commercial district to compete with other cities. Lying in the centre of the country almost

Advert for Humber Hillman cars, 1936.

Donald Gibson's vision for Coventry, 1945.

The city centre shopping precinct reaching completion in 1955.

equidistant from London and Manchester – both an hour away by train – and in the shadow of a resurgent Birmingham 30 kilometres up the road, its commercial office stock is generally outdated, limited and located piecemeal around the city. With both a university and polytechnic, and with Warwick University close by to the south, the city has an abundance of potential commercial growth and an incumbent research and development sector to tap into.

Our Friargate Masterplan is intentionally simple and direct. It reinforces the existing primary north/south routes and lines these with building plots; secondary routes east/west further divide these into more reasonable sizes; and tertiary connections feed and activate the whole. The resultant plots, which can be developed out in phases, contain active ground floors with commercial spaces at the upper levels. At the eastern and western edges the scale and heights of the buildings are reduced to relate to the surrounding city fabric and here, residential uses have been introduced. A newly defined transportation interchange between the rail and road connections is proposed to improve links with the rest of the country.

One of the most significant intentions has been to breach the ring road – this modern version of the city wall – and to reconnect the land beyond the city centre. The pedestrian route to and from the station is currently only semi-legible and, although relatively direct, involves negotiation of the inner ring road at junction six. Here the ring road itself is set within a deep cutting and the junction in the form of a large roundabout floats above it. The current

pedestrian routes by necessity are threaded under and through this knot of roads via subways and bridges.

With our encouragement Coventry City Council has taken the bold step to remove the existing roundabout, which will enable us to achieve the goal of a widened connection across the ring road. We have introduced a land bridge to a maximum permissible width without affecting the headroom of the dual carriageway underpass which has enabled us to extend Greyfriars Green southwards and link this to a new civic square in front of the station to the south. For us, the extraordinary achievement is to have removed what was seen as a permanent city fixture. In a city where the car has been king we have been able to demonstrate that it is after all possible to reverse time, to untie these knots and release the pressure to enable new development.

Opposite: Friargate masterplan drawing showing the new route connecting the station to the city centre across the ring road.

Planning without planners

Graham Morrison

Bankside's history has been one of expediency. Always on the edge of the city and never at its centre, it has been a servant and an appendage to London rather than being at its heart.

From its marshland beginnings, Bankside developed first as a market garden and a staging post at the river crossing, then as a depository for brewing, brothels, prisons, theatres, bear baiting and other less welcome but nonetheless essential activities of a thriving medieval city. The arrival of the railway in the nineteenth century saw the ruthless construction of viaducts, carrying goods and people from Kent and Sussex, by-passing Bankside at high level and connecting with the new river bridges and the city on the north bank. The twentieth century saw the construction of the massive Bankside power station providing electricity for the City of London.

Despite being geographically almost at the epicentre of one of the world's major cities, Bankside has been historically positioned, even as recently as the millennium, at the edge of things. It was never considered a good place to live or to work and in terms of significance to the capital, it has always been secondary.

As a place, it is characterised by buildings that are straightforward, direct and functional. It has no civic set pieces, no classical grand plan and no overt signs of wealth. Its urban fabric is dominated by two nineteenth-century interventions that contradicted the grain of its pre-Victorian street pattern. First the thoroughfare of Southwark Street was driven through the older matrix of streets and lanes to link London Bridge with Blackfriars Bridge and then the railway viaducts were overlain across the fabric and remain like deep defensive walls enclosing a medieval city. These interventions provoked some bold architectural responses but many of these were destroyed by the air raids in the Second World War.

Since the millennium, however, the fortunes of Bankside have been transformed. Four further, but more positive, urban interventions have given it new importance. First was the coming of the Jubilee Line with a new station at Southwark. Second was the decision of the Tate to move to the disused power station at Bankside. Third was the construction of the Millennium Bridge linking St Paul's and the City directly to the heart of Bankside. And fourth was the completion of the Southbank riverside walk. These new connections, together with the significance of Tate Modern have, for the first time, made Bankside a part of the city in its own right. Within a decade, Bankside's potential has been transformed from the limitations of being a servile urban adjunct to that of a well-connected, vibrant, purposeful and valuable part of London.

The two slab blocks of St Christopher's House, built in the 1960s, formed an impermeable barrier separating Southwark Street from the River Thames.

The advent of these new commercial opportunities had coincided with a withdrawal of resources from local government departments that left a planning vacuum. Planners could only react to applications and apply dubiously effective rules to limit height, proximity and uses and maintain daylighting standards. It was left to developers to make proposals and take responsibility for an evolving urban plan. In Bankside, as a result, urban design has become a reactive and iterative process rather than the product of a considered masterplan. It is proving an interesting experiment, and may lend credence to arguments for such non-prescriptive planning elsewhere. No responsible developer wants to see the value of their assets diminished by bad urban decisions. The quality of Bankside's streets and connections is as much in the landowners' interests as it is in those of the planners.

It is certainly extraordinary how one new intervention to secure a new urban link has been initiated and pursued within a series of adjacent and unrelated developments. This is the pedestrian route that links St Paul's Cathedral and Paternoster Square in the City of London with Union Street that defines the southern boundary of Bankside. The catalyst for this route was the Millennium Bridge. Opened first in 2000 (it reopened following structural alterations in 2002), it initiated the opening up of a new series of spaces linking the Cathedral with the river.

This new pedestrian bridge lands on the South Bank in front of Tate Modern. The success of the new gallery has in turn provoked a major extension on its south side that will include a new southern entrance giving access to its hinterland community.

This entrance will be open for perhaps sixteen hours each day allowing a public route through what would otherwise have been a huge impermeable industrial brick shell. This new southern entrance will open onto a new landscaped square.

To the south of this square a new commercial development now occupies the site of the previous St Christopher's House – the largest office building in Europe, when it was built in the 1960s. A single monolithic structure, it followed no particular building line, had no activity on its ground floor and, most significantly, along its entire 235 metre length, was completely impermeable. Its orthogonal geometry sat uncomfortably on the roughly triangular site, misaligned to its adjacent streets leaving awkward residual spaces to be used by parking space.

The demolition of this ungainly building provided the opportunity to redevelop the site, solve its inherent problems and continue the route from Tate Modern. Our masterplan for the three new buildings aimed to provide significantly more floor space, re-establish the street pattern, and provide activity on the ground floor. To the west, the building line was adjusted to provide visitors to Tate Modern with a clear line of sight to their destination. To the south, a wide tree-lined pavement rebalanced the dominance of the busily trafficked thoroughfare. But, most significantly, a new street – Canvey Street – divided the site into logical developable parcels and provided the link from Tate Modern to the north with Southwark Street to the south.

A new pedestrian crossing extends this route to the other side of the street. Here, at the entrance to Allies and Morrison's studios, a passage is formed where the overlap of the historic street pattern reduces the buildings depth to 6 metres. Beyond this a landscaped yard will connect the route to Lavington Street which opens to a further series of urban capillaries that reach Union Street on the south side of Bankside's enclosing viaduct.

The buildings are simple, direct and largely rectangular forms. Their varied orientations are taken from and reinforce the existing site geometries providing a series of distinctive external spaces. Their straightforward and legible organisation serves flexible, open floor plates placed above an animated ground floor. The detailing of these large flexible structures is modest and direct and resonates with the robust and uncomplicated compositions of the many Victorian warehouses that characterise the area.

Without any kind of masterplan, a new pedestrian route will be formed linking St Paul's Cathedral on the north bank with Union Street on the south. This 1.2 kilometre connection will be made possible through a series of individual initiatives in which one developer will link to the conclusion of the last. Each acknowledges the responsibility of participating in an iterative and evolving urban plan that brings value to their land but which also makes the city a better place.

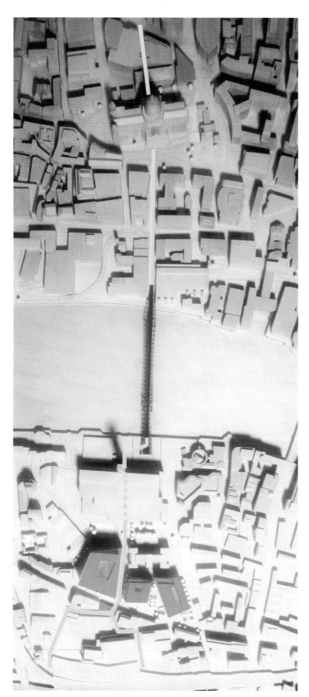

The new route connecting Bankside with St Paul's Cathedral and extending north into Union Street.

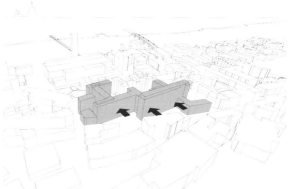

The previous St Christopher's House development, a series of self-referential slab blocks, restricted north–south movement.

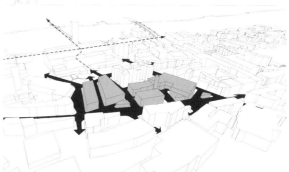

The new development opened up a network of routes.

The completed development.

Bankside 2 and 3.

Canvey Street: the new north–south route.

85 Southwark Street.

Farnham Place.

Hotel, Great Suffolk Street.

Student housing, Great Suffolk Street.

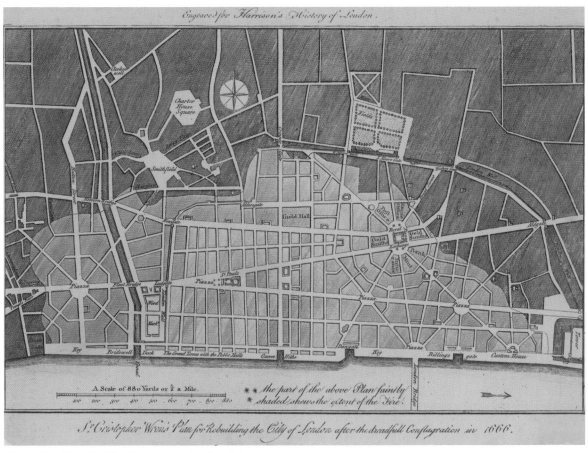

Plan for Rebuilding the City of London after the dreadful Conflagration, Sir Christopher Wren, 1666.

OBSERVATION   **The potential power of codes**

ANNO DECIMO NONO

CAROLI II. REGIS.

✸✸

CAP. III.

An Act for rebuilding the City of *London*.

FORASMUCH as the City of *London*, being the Imperial Seat of His Majesty's Kingdoms, and renowned for Trade and Commerce throughout the World, by reason of a most dreadful Fire lately happening therein was for the most Part thereof burnt down and destroyed within the Compass of a few Days, and now lies buried in its own Ruins: For the speedy Restoration whereof, and for the better Regulation, Uniformity, and Gracefulness of such new Buildings as shall be erected for Habitations, in order thereunto, and to the end that great and outrageous Fires (through the Blessing of Almighty God), so far forth as human Providence (with Submission to the Divine Pleasure) can foresee, may be reasonably prevented or obviated for the Time to come, both by the Matter and Form of such Building; and further, to the Intent that all Encouragement and Expedition may be given unto and all Impediments and Obstructions that may retard or protract the undertaking or carrying on a Work so necessary, and of so great Honour and Importance to His Majesty and this Kingdom and to the rest of His Majesty's Kingdoms and Dominions, may be removed:

II. Be it therefore enacted by the King's most Excellent Majesty, by and with the Advice and Consent of the Lords Spiritual and Temporal, and Commons, in this present Parliament assembled, and by the Authority of the same, That the Rules and Directions here-

A 2   after

---

4   19° CAROLI II. Cap.3.

after in this Act prescribed be duly observed by all Persons therein concerned.

Rules and Directions to be observed in building. III. And first, that no Building or House for Habitation whatsoever be hereafter erected within the Limits of the said City and Liberties thereof but such as shall be pursuant to such Rules and Orders of building and with such Materials as are herein-after particularly appointed, and according to such Scantlings as are set down and prescribed in a Table in this present Act hereafter specified; *Penalty.* and if any Person or Persons shall presume to build contrary thereunto, and be convicted of the same by the Oaths of Two or more credible Witnesses, to be taken before the Lord Mayor for the Time being, or any Two or more of the Justices of the Peace for the said City, who are hereby empowered to administer the same Oaths, that then and in such Case the said House so irregularly built as aforesaid shall be deemed as a common Nuisance, and the Builder and Levier thereof shall enter into a Recognizance in such Sum as the said Mayor and Justices respectively in their Discretions shall appoint, for Abatement and demolishing the same in convenient Time, or otherwise to amend the same according to such Rules and Orders as aforesaid; and in default of entering into such Recognizance the Offender shall be committed to the Common Gaol of the said City, there to remain without Bail or Mainprize till he shall have abated or demolished or otherwise amended the same, or else such irregular House shall or may be demolished or abated by Order of the Court of Aldermen.

Prevention of irregular Buildings. IV. And that the said irregular Buildings may be the better prevented or more effectually discovered, be it further enacted by the Authority aforesaid, *Lord Mayor, &c. to appoint Surveyors,* That the Lord Mayor, Aldermen, and Common Council of the said City shall and may, at their Will and Pleasure, elect, nominate, and appoint One or more discreet and intelligent Person or Persons in the Art of Building to be the Surveyors or Supervisors to see the said Rules and Scantlings well and truly observed; *and administer Oath.* and that it shall be lawful for the said Mayor, Aldermen, and Common Council, or for the Mayor and Aldermen in their Court of Aldermen, to administer to all the said Surveyors or Supervisors an Oath upon the Holy Evangelists, for the true and impartial Execution of their Office in that Behalf, and to appoint the several Precincts which shall be under their several Surveys.

There shall be Four Sorts of Buildings only. V. And to the end that all Builders may the better know how to provide and fit their Materials for their several Buildings, be it enacted, That there shall be only Four Sorts of Buildings, and no more, and that all manner of Houses so to be erected shall be of One of those Four Sorts of Buildings, and no other; (that is to say,) the First and least Sort of Houses fronting Bye Lanes, the Second Sort of Houses fronting Streets and Lanes of Note, the Third Sort of House fronting high and principal Streets, the Fourth and largest Sort of Mansion Houses for Citizens or other Persons of extraordinary Quality, not fronting either of the Three former Ways; and the Roofs of each of the said first Three Sorts of Houses respectively shall be uniform.

VI. And

An Act for rebuilding the City of London, 1667.

1667, London. In the aftermath of the Great Fire, two proposals are considered for rebuilding the City of London. One is a masterplan for the radical reconstruction of the city proposed by the architect Sir Christopher Wren. The other is a set of design codes or regulations which it was suggested should be applied to all reconstructed buildings devised by a committee which included Wren among its members.

Masterplans are relatively simple to produce but decidedly difficult to execute. It shouldn't be surprising then that it was the forty short codes – not the masterplan – which were adopted and which profoundly influence the way London looks today.

Unlike the masterplan, which had no sure route to implementation in the climate of debt, which prevailed at the time, the design codes offered an efficient and pragmatic mechanism to regulate expenditure, reduce costs and mitigate future risk to individual property owners. The rebuilding was paired with an economic mechanism which allowed rebuilding of public buildings and livery halls to commence quickly (a hypothecated levy on the import of coal into the City). In the process the medieval street pattern Wren had sought to erase was, of course, largely preserved.

The codes' influence extended well beyond their original purpose. The manner of building quickly spread to the provinces and colonies, such was their impact on architecture and urbanism. Indeed, the codes helped consolidate the style of architecture and urban practice we now think of as 'Georgian', though it was Charles II who was then on the throne.

Aerial view of Beirut. The site is 350 metres from Nejmeh Square, the heart of the city's beaux-arts radial plan.

District//S

Saifi North, Beirut

Two urban blocks in the heart of Beirut forming part of the government funded project to rebuild the centre of the war-damaged city. A series of discrete apartment buildings with shops at ground level frame a network of intimate external spaces.

In the aftermath of the 1975–1990 civil war, responsibility for the reconstruction of Beirut was given to Solidere, a government funded development agency. In some areas their work involved diligent restoration of historic fabric; in others it required comprehensive redevelopment for which a series of carefully composed urban rules were devised.

The District//S site occupies two urban blocks at the northern edge of the city centre, and was designated within the Solidere masterplan as an area of housing and shops. Although conceived as a single project, the aim was to create a complex, multi-layered urban environment.

One of the most recognisable characteristics of cities along the Mediterranean is the relaxed informality of their urbanism. The equable climate has always encouraged outdoor living, so that the spaces between buildings are as important as the buildings themselves. Buildings are often placed next to each other in an almost casual way giving shape to the most interesting and exciting spaces: tight little alleys, pocket *piazzas* and gardens. In most cases the character of these spaces is the consequence of ad-hoc growth over a long period of time. This scheme has tried to include that informality from the start.

The pedestrian routes within the new blocks have been designed to connect to the surrounding streets and neighbourhood. Within this network, the character of the routes are differentiated between those passing through the

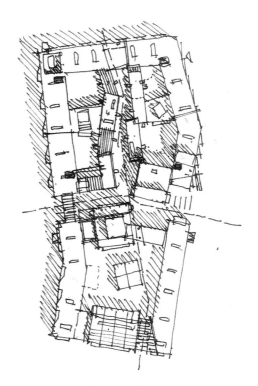

Early development sketch showing how perimeter buildings define the block shape. Pavilions informally occupy the interior and define a series of places.

central square and those meandering between small *piazzas* and overhanging gardens. Each building facade is composed to allow the ground floor spaces to actively address the street and maintain continuity of the street frontage.

The spaces have been composed to achieve both the best potential outlook for each flat, and to produce continuously unfolding views within the street. Each space is a perspectival composition, using the buildings to frame foreground elements and the middle distance to frame the view. The street walls with their balconies provide the frame and the detail. This essentially picturesque method of composing space has been carefully orchestrated so that there is always an important object or surface in the background that marks the destination.

All the apartments have a number of possibilities for outdoor living, both in the public spaces of the *piazzas*, lanes and gardens and also in private spaces: apartments have balconies and loggias, and the upper level penthouses have a roofscape of terraces, pools and gardens.

The buildings are simple. Making interesting places doesn't require buildings to be complex. Simple buildings are rational and flexible and will be able to adapt over time. Nearly all the buildings are conceived as straightforward rectangular volumes, changing in length and depth to accommodate the different types of apartments. The simple forms allow for efficient and straightforward floor plans. Only one deflects this geometry to deal with specific site

conditions. The shape of the buildings is regular, but they have been carefully placed on the plot to give complex and rich form to the spaces in between.

Every building in the masterplan follows the same compositional rule: a base, five-storeys of apartments and a varied top. This follows the traditional pattern of buildings in the historic centre of Beirut, as well as the requirements of Solidere's masterplan. It ties together the buildings within the same canon, whilst allowing for infinite variations in detail. The base accommodates commercial uses as well as entrances to the dwellings above. The five floors above provide the bulk of the residential accommodation, whilst the varied roofscape is created by the penthouse flats and pergolas.

Within this compositional rule, each building can find a unique combination of expression, colour and detail. Each should be recognisable as a home. The detail of the elevational treatments is derived from the historic architectural traditions of Beirut to create a family of elements. The architecture of this new quarter aspires to create a modern reinterpretation of key aspects of the traditional architecture of central Beirut in its scale, proximities, materials, details such as the windows and balconies and the animated skyline. Specific buildings are picked out to emphasise key points such as corners or end views.

Rather than having a consistent height across the site, the scheme has aimed to create a dynamic skyline.

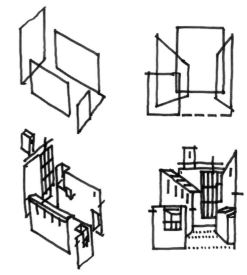

Study models were made of each of the spaces that the buildings formed.

Each view has three parts – a foreground, a middle and an eventful background.

View down pedestrian alley: timber
balconies in the background.

Loggias.

Arcades.

Balconies.

Fenestration.

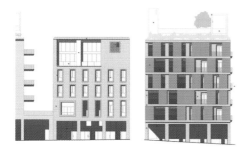

Following the sloping topography of the site, the buildings will effectively terrace from south to north. Above the sixth floor cornice line, a new world is created of penthouses with loggias and terraces. These forms introduce changes in height that will animate the skyline and give the opportunity to identify special landmark places.

Bottom left: A family of buildings is derived from an eight-storey typology. While the elevational composition of each of the twenty-two buildings is unique they are made from a common vocabulary of components.

Timber model showing the individual buildings and the network of public spaces they enclose. The ground floors open to a series of lanes, a square and a garden. The top floors are either villas or gardens with bridges connecting one with the other.

twenty two simple rectangular buildings...

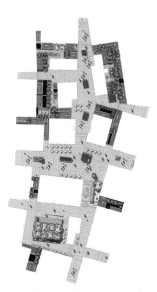

... produce complex spaces and a network of lanes, squares and gardens.

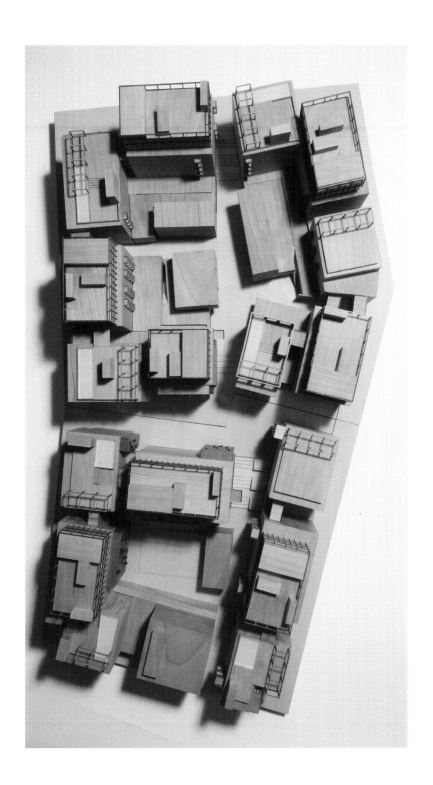

Alleys and lanes.

Shared garden spaces.

Defining the *piazza*.

The south-east street corner.

Terraces, roof gardens and rooftop pavilions.

Roof terrace villa.

Wolvercote Mill. A redundant industrial site on the edge of a
rural village.

Wolvercote Mill

Wolvercote, Oxfordshire

This proposal for the expansion of a small Oxfordshire village explored how the structure of the village – and in particular the relationship between its centre and its perimeter – might inform the pattern and hierarchy of the new development and influence its character and scale.

When Wolvercote, a small village outside Oxford, expanded in the middle years of the last century, a familiar suburban model was adopted with undifferentiated streets of semi-detached houses on individual plots. The pattern of the new housing bore no relationship to the form or structure of the older existing settlement, with its informal grouping of dwellings around a village green.

By contrast, our 2005 masterplan for Wolvercote Mill – a redundant industrial site formerly occupied by the Oxford University Press on the north-west corner of the village – attempted to relate the proposed new development explicitly both to the topography, scale and character of the village and to the complexity of the landscape setting, bounded by water meadows next to the River Isis, a tributary of the Thames. One of the key objectives of the plan was to use the site to create a new connection between the village and the surrounding countryside and let the buildings and spaces articulate the changing relationship between the two.

The brief for the masterplan came from the University who were concerned to expand the range and quality of family housing available to both staff and academics. The masterplan is conceived as a series of distinct building groupings each designed to relate specifically to its position on the site. So at the southern end of the site, the building form is more continuous and the variety of uses is greater – workspace and community as well as residential. Against the river, ponds and mill stream, the buildings follow a more linear pattern as they stand along the quayside. In the centre of the site, a group of differently configured buildings provide the enclosure to a central green. At the northern end of the site the disposition of the buildings becomes more informal and fragmented, while the central road gradually changes its character before turning into a country footpath. And on the eastern edge of the site, where the new development abuts the earlier "suburban" housing, a tighter pattern of gravelled courtyards provides the locus for groups of larger houses, the alignment of the individual dwellings (north/south or east/west) reflecting which side of the courtyard they occupy and therefore the orientation of their gardens.

While the masterplan was primarily concerned with the disposition of the different buildings and spaces, it was always assumed that the distinctions described would also be reflected in the character of the architecture of the individual buildings. The resulting richness and diversity would, it was hoped, provide the new development with a more complex and ambiguous character, blurring the division between the new and old and easing what would be a substantial volume of new housing into the relatively fragile setting of the existing village.

Meadow Lane: three-bedroom terrace housing defining the existing lane.

Mill Road entrance to site: offices and apartments enclosing a public green.

Canalside flats and houses along the re-opened culvert.

Family houses grouped around a shared courtyard.

Physical model showing the hierarchy of different places created within the masterplan reflected in the different housing typologies.

Aerial view of the BBC site showing the pre-existing headquarters
building and the linear blocks of the White City housing estate to
the west.

BBC Media Village

London

Rather than build an isolated corporate headquarters, this project for the BBC proposed an extension to the city, with a series of new urban blocks framing a sequence of public routes and spaces linked directly back to the adjacent residential neighbourhood.

The BBC selected White City as the site for its new headquarters in the mid-1980s. The first structure it built was a large, and somewhat prosaic, freestanding office building arranged around an external light well. Placed apparently arbitrarily on a diagonal in the middle of the plot–it in fact followed the alignment of the White City stadium that previously occupied the site–the new building stood within a field of car parking and some residual landscaping, entirely mute in its response to the adjacent streets, and isolated from the various communities that surrounded it.

By the late 1990s this degree of separation, and the sense of corporate aloofness that it implied, seemed increasingly at odds with the BBC's aspirations to engage more openly with the public that it served and from whom it received its funding.

The concurrent need to increase the amount of accommodation on the site provided a timely opportunity therefore to transform the relationship of the BBC with the surrounding city.

In complete contradiction of an earlier feasibility study commissioned by the BBC in which all the new

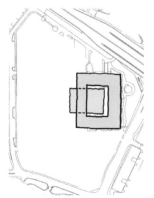

Direct connection opened up between the courtyard in the centre of the existing building and this new public space.

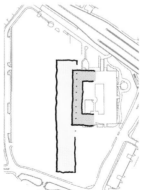

At the centre of the site a primary public space provides the focus for the new development.

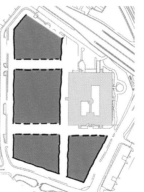

A clear urban structure embraces the existing building.

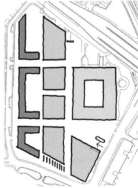

Perimeter buildings face out to the existing street.

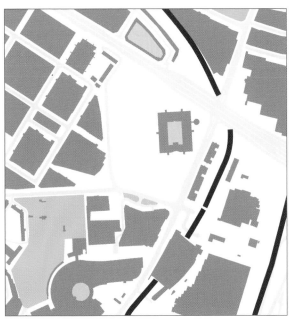

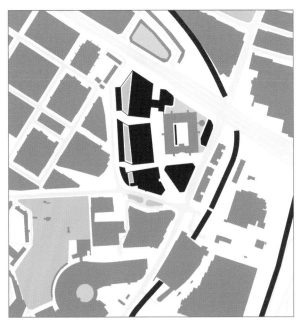

BBC Media Village: urban fabric as existing.

BBC Media Village: urban fabric as proposed.

accommodation was concentrated in a single building arranged around an internal street, our proposal – selected through competition – treated the project not as an architectural proposition but as an urban masterplan. The site was reconceived as a series of urban blocks which in turn framed a sequence of public spaces. As well as transforming the environment for those who work at the BBC, the new streets also introduced across the site a network of pedestrian routes connecting back directly into the surrounding residential area and making the entire site accessible to the general public.

At ground level – unlike the existing building – the new buildings were designed to face out rather than in so as to allow shops, cafes and restaurants to activate the new public spaces and provide new facilities and amenities not just for the BBC staff but for local residents. In the past all such facilities had been located on the interior of the BBC's buildings: now they were placed in the common domain and made available to everyone. The success of this approach was evidenced by the turnover of the supermarket that moved in and which proved to be one of the company's highest trading outlets.

While the plans of the individual buildings are relatively simple, the way they are configured on the site is more complex. Rather than adopt the orthogonal geometry of

the existing office, the new buildings splay out and pull back as they move from south to north across the site. Partly this is to maximise the area of new public space created, partly to acknowledge the significance of the new east–west connection to the White City Estate, and partly it allowed the balance of the space to change from being a street to a place of assembly, not unlike an English market town, where the main highway progressively widens to allow space for traders and their stalls. The landscape of the new public spaces was designed with Christopher Bradley-Hole who also designed individual gardens relating to each of the new buildings.

The first phase of development involved the construction of a new energy centre and two major new buildings containing office and production space. A further two large sites were allocated within the masterplan for additional BBC buildings, potentially including a new rehearsal space for the BBC orchestras.

In addition to the buildings required for the BBC's own use – which tend to face towards the centre of the site – a series of separate, smaller studio office buildings faced in brick were introduced on the perimeter to ensure that the surrounding streets are always addressed by the fronts of buildings and not by backs, creating a safe and friendly pedestrian environment.

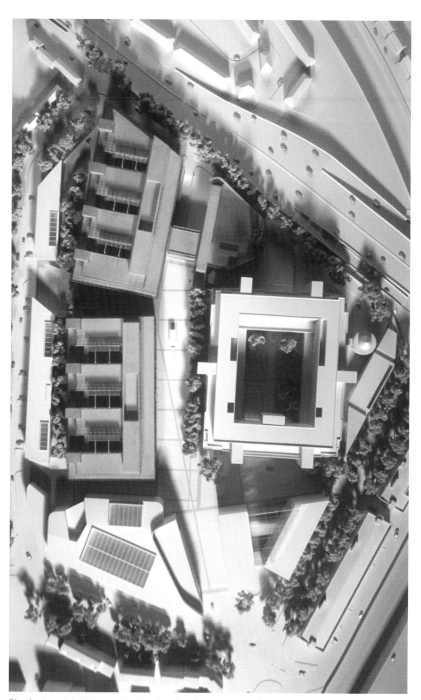

Physical model of the masterplan showing the sequence of new
public spaces.

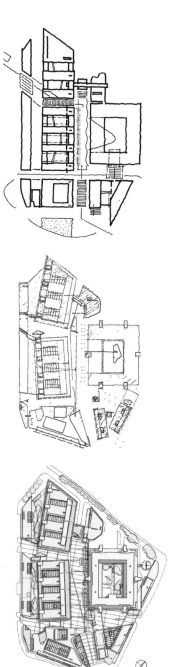

Early sketches showing evolution
of masterplan from a formal to an
informal building grouping.

Public open space between the new and existing.

New street frontage on the perimeter of the site.

Cross-street leading into the site.

The public space at night.

The residential perimeter block: principles, problems and particularities

Paul Eaton

The perimeter block remains for us the most useful and valid starting point for the residential components of our masterplans. There are of course myriad ways of composing urban form, each with their own merits or disadvantages in any given situation. But even when proposing alternative forms, we regard the perimeter block as a model against which these can be developed, tested and understood. Why has this model remained so compelling, and what are its limits?

Spaces

A perimeter block is an urban form that concentrates the development of a city block along its outermost–or public–edges. A number of important consequences flow from this. Perhaps the most significant is that it reinforces and makes clear the underlying pattern of privately owned plots, streets and public spaces that constitute the city. But it is not simply a question of clarity. By strongly defining their edges, perimeter blocks enable the streets and squares of a city to be thought of as positive spaces, as urban rooms. And by placing commercial uses in direct contact with this public realm, the perimeter block provides the best possible opportunity for contact and exchange.

But external space in cities is not always public. Because the depths of buildings are defined by the need for adequate daylight, the perimeter plan naturally produces an open space at its centre. This space has no obligation to be public and–in many cases is best not to be so. In traditional perimeter blocks–those containing a number of different land ownerships–this space is usually allocated to private gardens, yards and ancillary buildings. In schemes where a single development encompasses an entire urban block, this central space is more often given over to a variety of communal functions: play spaces, gardens, cycle parking. In either case, the perimeter block typology promotes an explicit distinction between the private or communal realm and the public realm. This absence of ambiguity is important. Each type of use has its own 'rules' of behaviour and, importantly, its own maintenance regimes. Other typologies that produce more ambiguous patterns can be hard to make work. The forlorn and unclaimed land that surrounds many stand-alone post-war housing blocks are obvious examples of ill-defined communal space.

Composition

The structure of towns and cities tends to be hierarchical. Just as there are grand squares, high streets and parks, so there are back streets, side streets, narrow lanes

Leslie Martin's diagram explaining the benefit of perimeter planning. The area of the perimeter frame is equal to the area of the square it encloses.

Charles Rowan House, Islington, London.

This inter-war perimeter block exhibits a clear contrast between an informal communal courtyard space that plays host to the paraphernalia of day-to-day life (right) and its distinctive but comparatively mute urban frontages (left).

and alleys. Each urban block necessarily has to form its own set of relationships within this wider urban matrix – its own fronts, backs and sides, its own particular aspects and prospects. Because they are usually large in plan but still able to be conceived as a series of discrete pieces, perimeter blocks allow a certain looseness of composition. Unlike the free-standing pavilion building which must conform to a single coherent architectural composition, the perimeter block is a type that is fundamentally well disposed to respond to its place in the city fabric. Each side of a block can adopt a form, scale and character suited to the street or space that it addresses. No matter how secondary the frontage of a perimeter block may be, it always defines a street frontage.

Because the perimeter block makes a clear distinction between these fronts and their corresponding backs, their rear elevations – relieved of any obligation to play a wider role within the city – are able to develop a more ad hoc character in response to specific uses or the nature of the central courtyard space. While this distinction is more evident in traditional mixed ownership blocks – in the tenements of nineteenth-century Edinburgh for example – and even more so where these contain a mix of uses, this conceptual framework can still provide opportunities for architectural expression within single ownership blocks. This fundamental flexibility also enables a variety of different building uses to be incorporated within a normative urban pattern. Large scale/deep plan uses such as car parking – whether below ground or beneath a podium – is the most common of these, but large retail units, energy centres, schools, health facilities and even offices can similarly be incorporated.

Efficiency
Lastly, the perimeter block also offers a solution to the efficient use of land, a point made by Leslie Martin in his 1972 essay "The grid as a generator: exploration of a new theoretical framework for the use of land in cities".[1] Martin noted that density need not be equated with tall buildings, pointing out that for a given area of land, a courtyard form would achieve the same density as a tower form of three times the height. While this argument ultimately led Martin to advocate the development of large mixed-use super blocks where the block interior is public, such as Patrick Hodgkinson's Brunswick Centre, 1965–1973, it also provided justification for projects such as the residential courtyard block at Clipstone Street designed by Michael Gold for Frederick Macmanus and Partners, 1966–1971, and remains relevant to any reasonably sized perimeter development.

1. Martin, L, "The grid as a generator: exploration of a new theoretical framework for the use of land in cities", in *Urban Space and Structures*, Cambridge: Cambridge University Press, 29 May 1975.

Clipstone Street, Fitzrovia, London.

A rare example of a single ownership perimeter block from the 1970s. Its exterior character (left) is somewhat at odds with its surrounding context and instead has more in common with the bright white interior elevations. Undercroft car parking and a nursery school lie below the communal garden.

Density and quality

The efficient use of land and the maximisation of density have become increasingly important issues in contemporary urban planning. In London, according to the Greater London Authority, projected population rises mean as many as fifty thousand new homes are needed every year. It is perhaps unsurprising then that in the city's identified growth areas – typically on former industrial land on the edges of the city centre or in the Thames Gateway corridor – the residential densities proposed are significantly higher than those in the surrounding areas, with over four hundred dwellings per hectare being not uncommon.

Alongside – and partly in reaction to – these strategies for growth, new planning policies and guidance have emerged that reflect a growing concern for the quality of newly built residential accommodation, including requirements for minimum internal floor areas, private amenity spaces and communal external space and, perhaps most importantly in the context of high density development, for daylight, sunlight, and natural ventilation levels within flats. These changes are overwhelmingly positive. Setting aside the complexities of housing affordability and stability of tenure, creating homes that are genuinely fit for purpose, that people like and therefore want to live in, is arguably the best way to encourage the kind of stability and social cohesion more traditionally found in neighbourhoods of houses.

New forms

In recent years this tension between increasing density and raising standards has prompted the development of a number of different types of perimeter block. At a height of between three and six-storeys perimeter blocks remain low enough to ensure adequate sunlight and daylight to both the courtyard and the blocks interior elevations. But as densities increase and building heights rise, this becomes impossible to achieve without manipulating the basic perimeter block form in some way.

City block, Fitzrovia, London.

Just to the north of Clipstone Street, this more typical London perimeter block contains a number of separate ownerships, buildings and uses. Georgian terraced houses, an Edwardian mansion block and 1980s housing form the perimeter (left), while a small church and gardens lie at its centre (right).

These manipulations can involve either breaking the block in plan, or stepping down in section, or both. Perhaps the most striking departure from the basic type is seen in the hybrid perimeter block and tower arrangement, which, in a rebuttal to Martin's argument, explores whether it might be possible to have both. These hybrid forms are characterised by a perimeter block from which one or more taller elements rise. At the corners they may either be free-standing or integrated into the form and architecture of the base block. A second type is the stepped block, where building heights rise and fall around the perimeter in response to orientation – either to admit southern light into the courtyard or prevent overshadowing on its northern edge – an approach which, if pursued to its logical extreme would invariably generate parallel rows of north-south orientated buildings, antithetical, very often, to the urban condition in which they are located.

The tension therefore now pulls three ways – between quality and quantity – and also urban clarity. In reconciling density with quality, we need to be careful not to undermine the spatial clarity and continuity of the city fabric and to acknowledge the reciprocal nature of the relationship between the configuration of urban form and nature of the public domain.

Aerial view of the Brent Cross Cricklewood site bisected by the
North Circular Road.

Brent Cross Cricklewood

London

An out-of-town shopping centre built in the 1960s next to London's North Circular Road is reintegrated into the fabric of the city that surrounds it as part of a proposal for a new metropolitan centre served by a new railway station and including up to seven thousand five hundred new homes.

In addition to the significance of its strategic location – positioned at the southern end of the M1 on the junction with the North Circular Road, bordered by the A41 to the east and the Edgware Road to the west, edged by the Midland Mainline railway on its western boundary and within striking distance of the Northern Line on the east – what made this site unusual, and perhaps unique in London, was a combination of three further factors. The first was its size: it covers an area of 151 hectares. The second was its proximity to central London: it is situated just 8 kilometres from the West End. And the third was the comparative absence across the site of any major constraints that would inhibit the nature, scale and density of any future development.

When you look back at the history of the site it is clear that it has been dominated by the presence of strategic transport infrastructure – and its consequences – since the second half of the nineteenth century when the railways were first overlaid across what had until then been agricultural land. This was followed between the wars, by the construction of the North Circular Road and, in 1977, by the completion of the Staples Corner junction with the M1.

Where new roads go, so industry tends to follow and by 1929 fifty-seven factories had taken up position in the area of Staples Corner. It was of course for precisely the same reason that this site was chosen, in the 1960s, for the erection of the Brent Cross Shopping Centre, London's first 'out-of-town' shopping mall.

One of the ironies of this surfeit of transport infrastructure is that in many respects it is easier to get to Brent Cross if you are arriving by car from another part of London than it is if you live locally and want to travel on foot or by bike. Neither is it in any sense an easy, or a pleasant, journey if you are making your way there from the nearest underground station, on the other side of the A41. It is also true that the various roads and railways that surround the site, as well as all the associated car parks and service yards, have left the existing community isolated and separated from the adjacent neighbourhoods. Any sense of an urban continuum, of a consistent matrix of roads and buildings, has been lost entirely.

The masterplan is intended to remedy all of these problems, partly by forging new connections across these various barriers and partly by establishing a coherent urban framework capable of binding all the disparate areas of the site together. At the heart of the new plan is the proposal to create at Brent Cross Cricklewood what will in effect be a new town centre spanning both sides of the North Circular Road. The existing shopping facilities of Brent Cross – supplemented by additional retail space, cinemas, hotels and housing – will be linked via three new bridges to a new commercial and residential community on the south side of the road. In total the new development will provide approximately seven thousand five hundred homes and workspace for up to forty thousand people.

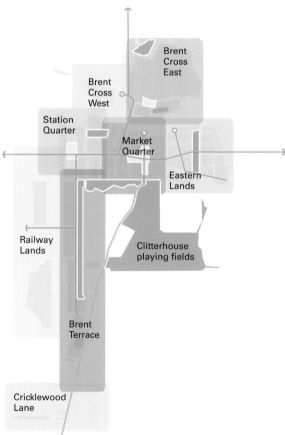

Plan showing the overlapping relationship between different neighbourhoods, each with their own character.

Key to the realisation of this new town centre is the decision to construct, as part of the Thameslink 2000 project, a new main line station on the southern part of the site with the capacity to accommodate twelve car trains and provide a service of eight trains per hour. For Brent Cross what this new station offers, together with associated plans for improved local bus services and easier and more direct pedestrian and cycle connections to

Brent Cross underground station, is a far more sustainable future, one in which there will be a new emphasis on public transport and a reduced dependence on the private car.

In turn, the existing shopping centre, by way of reciprocation, offers a huge attraction and resource for the new development, a real amenity for those who come to live and work there. And as part of the overall masterplan the shopping centre, originally designed as an inward-looking

EDGWARE ROAD

Brent Cross
Shopping Centre

NORTH CIRCULAR ROAD

new
station

new
bridge

HENDON WAY

Clitterhouse
playing fields

Brent Cross Cricklewood,
illustrative masterplan.

Typical street in the new
residential quarter.

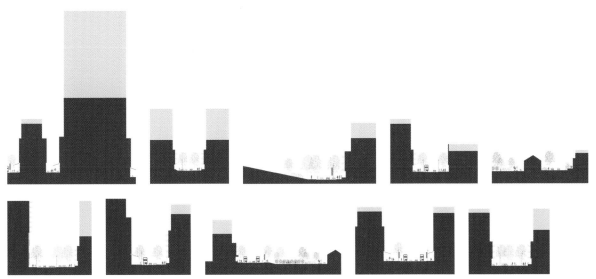

Cross-section diagrams illustrating the character and scale of different streets and spaces.

mall, isolated from the outside world, will itself turn to face south to establish a new waterside setting along a realigned and exposed River Brent, and a new bus interchange.

While in terms of transport, and movement, and activity, the connection between the new station and Brent Cross is key, the primary structure on the south side is the east–west street, which links the new main line station to Brent Cross underground station. This is deliberately designed as an informal street, which undergoes changes in its character throughout its length, moving from the most intensive section around the new main line station where the main office uses will be focussed, through to the Market Square which will act as the neighbourhood shopping centre, and finally into the more predominantly residential areas of the Eastern Lands.

Underpinning the masterplan is a matrix of roads, squares, streets and lanes which both establish the disposition of the urban blocks and define patterns of movement through the site – pedestrian, cycle, and vehicular. Implicit within this matrix is a clear urban hierarchy that emphasises the primary significance of key routes – such as the east-west street that links the new main line station to Brent Cross underground or the north–south road that follows the linear park – while at the same time acknowledging the subordinate role and character of the smallest lanes.

The overall configuration of the roads has been planned to allow long-term flexibility in the way that vehicular/pedestrian/cycle movement is managed across the site, but an initial proposition has been made which directs vehicular movement onto specific routes and dedicates substantial sections of the network exclusively for pedestrian, cycle and, in certain cases, public transport use.

In the past, the conventional approach in projects of this scale has been to allow the hierarchy of traffic movement to act as the determinant of the urban form. The Brent Cross Cricklewood masterplan avoids this and instead encourages traffic simply to utilise the relevant part of the urban matrix. As a result the tendency is for streets and spaces to vary in character throughout their length, sometimes busy with cars and buses, sometimes enjoying the quiet of exclusive pedestrian use.

The masterplan sets out the location of all the main streets, squares and roads and in so doing establishes the shape and configuration of the main development parcels. But the planning application also contains a series of parameter plans which define such aspects as the nature and hierarchy of the public spaces; the quantum of different uses within each of the development parcels and what uses are permissible at both ground and upper levels; the maximum heights of buildings both on frontages and within the centres of the blocks; the obligations to build up to building lines; the permitted location of underground structures and where access to these underground may be located.

In order to assess these parameters a number of key sites were tested early in the process with the help of other architects – Maccreanor Lavington, Buschow Henley, Patrick Lynch, DRMM and PRP. In order to explain them, case studies were also prepared for the local authority showing how the parameters, and the associated design guidelines, would provide sufficient control over the character and configuration of individual buildings as they came forward.

...*exploit*
**THE POTENTIAL
OF THE PRE-EXISTING**

...*prioritise*
**SPACE OVER
FORM**

...*provide*
**A CLEAR
HIERARCHY**

The history and topography of a site are important, not only because they help explain the nature of its past, but because they can inform the shape of its future.

In Japanese calligraphy the space formed by the brushstroke is as important as the shape of the line: in a masterplan the focus must be as much on the space between buildings as it is on the buildings themselves.

Cities are easier to understand, and therefore easier to use, when their urban structure conforms to a hierarchy, because it is this that defines and discloses the relative significance of its constituent parts.

OBSERVATION   **A masterplan should...**

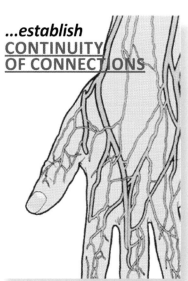

...establish
**CONTINUITY
OF CONNECTIONS**

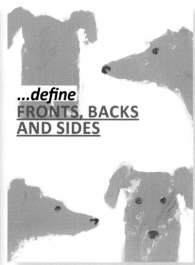

...define
**FRONTS, BACKS
AND SIDES**

...accommodate
**THE REALITY
OF THE PRESENT**

In an urban plan, the making – or re-making – of connections is essential to establishing a continuum between the existing city and the new.

A masterplan should both set out the rules that define the nature of the urban fabric and make clear the role that each building is expected to play within it.

If a masterplan is to be realised it must propose buildings that people want to build today. Structures whose plans, shapes, uses or locations are inappropriate or contrived will deter investment rather than attract it.

These posters, prepared as part of an exhibition held at the British School at Rome in October 2010, combined images and slogans to explain some of the key principles we follow in the preparation of our masterplans. Without attempting to be exhaustive or exclusive, the exhibition identified some of the critical issues that a masterplan, and particularly an urban masterplan, has to address.

...provide
A SURROGATE CONTEXT

...acknowledge
THE UNCERTAINTIES OF THE FUTURE

...create
COMPLEX SPACES WITH SIMPLE BUILDINGS

In the absence of an established context, a masterplan offers a virtual setting within which individual buildings can be designed and against which they can be judged.

Cities are not static and buildings change over time. A masterplan which ignores this, which fails to accommodate the processes of demolition and replacement, may not only become an obstacle to change but may, at some stage, become an agent of decline.

It is much easier to achieve complexity and richness within a masterplan by manipulating the relationships between buildings than to achieve it by forcing the shape and configuration of the buildings themselves.

...promote
DIFFERENCE AND DIVERSITY

...look
OUT NOT IN

...describe
A PROCESS NOT A PRODUCT

The job of the masterplan is to provoke and encourage not to constrain and prescribe. What unites a masterplan is the consistency of its structure not the limitations imposed on its aesthetics.

Too many contemporary masterplans are so self-absorbed in their vision for the interiors of their sites that they fail to address the often much more significant, and much more difficult, issues pertaining to their edges.

A masterplan is not a rigid architectural proposition, it is a flexible, informal and open-ended definition of relationships that must be expected to evolve and change as it is implemented. The presence of a single all-encompassing order–often so essential to the design of a building–is irrelevant to the design of a masterplan.

Doha, 1947. The old Msheireb district developed to the right of the fort.

Msheireb

Doha

Masterplanned by AECOM and Arup, the Msheireb Downtown Doha development represents a pioneering attempt to establish a new type of urban quarter within the centre of a Middle Eastern city. Rather than rely on generic models drawn from elsewhere – towers, plazas, freeways – the Msheireb plan deploys forms of spatial organisation and architectural expression more specific to the particular character of the city and its climate.

The role we were given within the development of the Msheireb masterplan was to propose its architectural characteristics and then, through a combination of models, diagrams, perspectives and worked examples, to convey these to the architects responsible for the hundred individual buildings planned for this 35 hectare site.

Alongside the worked examples, a design manual was compiled as part of a wider suite of Master Development Standards. The purpose of the Architecture section was both to tell the story of the project's link with Qatari traditions and to suggest ways in which continuity could be established with contemporary building types, alongside a wider effort to realign the contemporary Islamic city with more culturally resonant and sustainable forms. A number of traditional urban typologies were used, for example, as springboards for transformation – the *fireej*, an extended family cluster of dwellings around a communal space with a *majlis*, or guest reception room; the courtyard house comprising one such dwelling or multiplying out at a larger scale into a palace complex; the *souk*, a hybrid of building and covered street; and the *sikka*, a narrow alleyway that can broaden into a *baraha*, or informal square.

The architectural objectives of the project were summarised in the "Seven Steps", a manifesto intended to define a new language of architecture for Msheireb. These emphasised continuity and resonance with the massing and articulation of traditional Qatari architecture; a

high degree of material consistency between buildings by diverse architects and their grouping together to reflect the informal, 'moulded' character of the traditional and compact Islamic city; the creation of shade at street level, active rooftops, courtyards and terraces, using building form, colonnades and overhangs to promote external comfort and walk-ability; and the articulation of deep, layered facades, designed to minimise solar gain, in combination with natural ventilation and building systems to achieve maximum internal comfort with minimum energy use.

The first group of buildings to be completed will be the Diwan Amiri Quarter for which we were separately appointed as architects. The design evolution of the Diwan Amiri Quarter both influenced, and was influenced by, the parallel development of the wider masterplan. This overlap enabled detailed aspects of the emerging architectural language to be fed into the design guidelines for other phases, adding a richness and depth to the documentation.

The irregular shape of the Diwan Amiri Quarter site stems from the retention of three historic courtyard houses, and this street pattern generated the disposition of the buildings: the Diwan Annexe offices at the west end, facing the southern axis of the Amiri Diwan (seat of government); the Guards building at the centre, controlling the security of the site, and the National Archive at the east, facing the *corniche* and the *souk*. The inspiration for the architectural language of each of the distinct uses was found in three

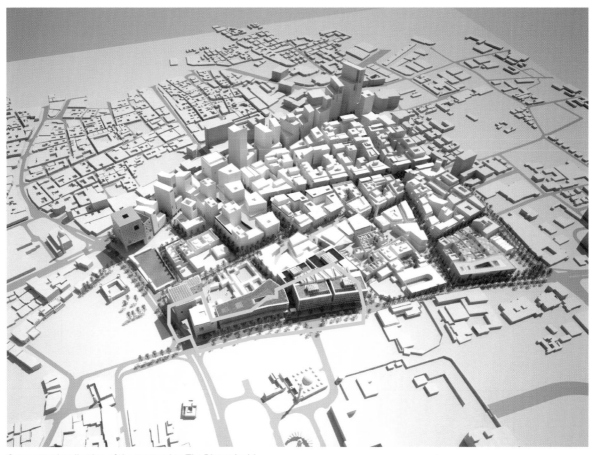

Computer visualisation of the masterplan. The Diwan Amiri
Quarter is outlined in yellow.

archetypal Qatari building types: the arcaded *diwania*, or
small palace, for the Diwan Annexe; the courtyard dwelling
and military fort for the Guards residence; and the fortified
watchtower for the Archive.

The Annexe is organised as a cluster of four buildings
linked by bridges, each with its own internal courtyard,
grouped around a central, top-lit 'covered street'. This
space reinterprets the tradition of the shaded *souk* to
form both a ground level gathering place and routes at
the upper levels in the form of colonnaded galleries. Like
its precedent, this common area between the offices has
an ambiguous outside/inside character, stone clad, cool,
proportionally narrow and tall, and lit by minimal diffused
light from above.

The route connects across an entrance yard to the
Guards building where it expands into a large, external
courtyard, shaded by a cantilevered canopy. As with the
traditional Qatari house the courtyard forms the central
reference point for the organisation of the Guard's private
rooms at the perimeter. The irregular geometry of the

deeply articulated stone clad walls – traces of the old
town and its climate responsive vernacular tradition – is
contrasted with a simple rectangle cut out of the bronze
panelled canopy overhead.

The National Archive is arranged in three parts to form a
set of interconnected public spaces that fold around the
heritage houses, now being restored as museums, to
form part of a wider heritage quarter. The archive storage
tower is a prominent landmark and a symbol of the
regeneration of the downtown area of the city whilst the
entrance hypostyle frames both the long scale view to
the *souk* and the intimate scale of the courtyard house,
establishing an ambiguous relationship between the
house as an artefact, the archiving of Qatar's domestic
traditions and their contemporary civic context.

A grand colonnade addressing the old Diwan and the
ceremonially significant Al Rayyan Road to the North
unites the facades of the three buildings. The colonnade
designs of the individual buildings differ within a set of
common parameters, allowing each to make their own

Arcaded facades (*liwan*) characterise the traditional Qatari palace.

The Jalmood House is typical of the traditional Qatari courtyard house.

Fortified watchtowers provided places of safety between the desert and the sea.

Diwan Annexe entrance area and layered facade.

Amiri Guards south facade.

National Archive and Heritage House.

Covered street at the heart of the Diwan Annexe.

Diwan Annexe and Amiri Guard colonnades.

Continuity of exterior finishes into the primary interior spaces.

distinctive contribution to the whole. In a similar way, but at a smaller scale, each building is elaborated by a unique palette of bespoke patterns, derived from the natural and cultural history of Qatar. These add a narrative element, pertinent to each building type, but are strictly controlled to particular building elements – the inner lining of entrances for example – subservient to the primary order of walls and openings.

During the construction of the Diwan Amiri Quarter, designs for all the remaining buildings within the masterplan's four phases were developed by a diverse group of architects, reviewed, and approved by the client and masterplan team on the basis of compliance with the masterplan standards.

The Diwan Amiri Quarter is both an exposition of the "Seven Steps" manifesto for a new, site-specific Qatari architecture and a microcosm of the wider Msheireb Downtown Doha masterplan.

Overleaf: Entrance courtyard.

Density and its virtues:
what is our residential footprint?

Bob Allies and Paul Eaton

In Britain, in the last century, most discussions of urban, or suburban, development – certainly since the passing of the Town and Country Planning Act in 1947 – typically regarded density as a threat. Design proposals which appeared to maximise, in terms of area, the development potential of a site were invariably criticised as being "too dense", a threat to established notions of scale, privacy or character.

But as we move further into the twenty-first century and as we cope with the consequences of a world in which we are competing for an ever-diminishing supply of space and resources, density, or more accurately, increased density, is becoming acknowledged as an essential prerequisite for sustainability.

Today we need to build more compactly – to live and work more closely together – because it is only in this way that we can reduce the need for our towns and cities to expand and therefore limit our impact on the surrounding land. Concentrating development allows us to minimise our need for transport and therefore be more effective in our consumption of energy. It also makes it easier to provide the range of resources and facilities needed to support a vital social and cultural life and to ensure their long-term viability.

Of course, high-density living does not come without some potential disadvantages. Lack of privacy, reduced amenity space, close proximity to neighbours, restricted sunlight and daylight, shortage of storage, overshadowing and overlooking are all problems that may result from high-density development, while questions will always be raised as to its appropriateness as a setting in which to bring up children.

Therefore while current planning policy in London, for example, does now encourage density – particularly in relation to major transport nodes – such proposals are still widely viewed with suspicion.

Nevertheless, as the concern of policy makers changes from whether projects are too dense to whether they are dense enough, so the accuracy of our assessment of density becomes increasingly important. It might even, at some point, be appropriate to be able to reward, or compensate, those living at higher densities – and therefore occupying less land and requiring a smaller share of public services – by for example lowering their level of taxation, just as different categories of vehicles are taxed according to their fuel efficiency.

Calculations of residential density have conventionally related numbers of people, or dwellings, or habitable rooms, to the area of the site. These simple ratios, however, fail to acknowledge many critical aspects of a development. They do not, for example,

$$f = \frac{(a-b)\, c}{100d}$$

residential footprint

f = residential footprint
a = total site area
b = area of site dedicated to public use
c = percentage of gross development
    area allocated to residential use
d = number of occupants

take into account areas allocated to other uses such as retail, car parking, transport, or workspace. They do not reflect the extent to which areas of the site have been opened up as public realm rather than retained for private, or communal, use. And they ignore the impact of neighbouring land uses – of areas of open space, parks, riverside or sea front. In short, they disregard the qualitative consequences of density, how it actually feels on the ground.

Of these omissions, the latter is perhaps the most difficult to address as opinion will inevitably divide as to the merit, or justification, of taking off-site land uses into account. But a measure of residential density that reflects both the proportion of the site area allocated to the public and the proportion of the development area allocated to other uses might be possible.

Just as we can measure an individual's carbon footprint, so it would seem helpful if – as part of the documentation of a development project – we were able to establish what share of the site area is effectively being allocated to each new resident, to define, in other words, what will be the "residential footprint", measured in metres squared, of each person living within the scheme.

What is considered an appropriate residential footprint will vary according to its location, and in particular in relation to its proximity to other facilities – shops, transport, schools. But in principle the smaller our residential footprint, the less land we occupy and the more sustainable we are.

In order to assess the residential footprint of an individual, we need to relate the area of the site (excluding any land retained for public use), firstly to the proportion of the total development allocated to residential use and secondly to the number of inhabitants expected to occupy it. This can be calculated using the formula shown here.

Applied to a typical three-storey London terraced house occupied by a family of five, with a small front garden and a 10 metre deep rear garden, a calculation of the residential footprint of each occupant is likely to be around 30 square metres.

In contrast, if this formula is applied to the projects illustrated in this book, all of them achieve significantly lower residential footprints ranging from 17.9 square metres per occupant for Wolvercote, to 4.8 square metres for St Andrews Bow, and as low as 1.8 square metres at Aldgate Place.

Wood Wharf, London, located immediately to the east of
Canary Wharf on the Isle of Dogs.

Wood Wharf, Canary Wharf

London

Set in the context of some of the highest density development in London, this masterplan extends the dynamic, but homogeneous, financial centre of Canary Wharf with a more complex, mixed-use quarter containing a variety of residential, retail, and office uses on the edge of a neighbouring wharf.

Its form the result of two centuries of shipping evolution within the historic docklands, Wood Wharf today feels like an island, entirely unaffected by more than two decades of continuous development at the adjacent Canary Wharf. The aim of the masterplan is to overcome its insular character and achieve three further goals.

First it must be a natural and compatible extension of Canary Wharf itself, reinforcing its neighbour's significance and introducing a greater variety of uses. Second it must generate a series of familiar spaces – streets, squares and gardens – that will make it a part of London as much as it is a part of Canary Wharf: it must, in other words, integrate its new urban fabric with that which already exists. And third it must become a place in its own right, strongly characterful in itself, but exploiting the essential characteristics of its site – its history, its waterfront and its scale.

The masterplan is not a vision for the future, it is a street pattern. Where earlier masterplans for the same site relied on single, primary gestures – a major park (Rogers), a long curving boulevard (Farrell) – this masterplan is founded more directly on straightforward urban principles. It is flexible so as to allow each plot to be capable of being occupied by a number of different uses and typologies. Its public spaces are distributed so that each residential plot is adjacent to either a park or water and its commercial plots front the major streets that are in turn a part of a familiar urban hierarchy. It has a series of public spaces – a

market place, a main square, a London park – all connected with a network of footpaths that connect the Grade I listed basin to the north with the informal park to the south and the existing community to the east with Canary Wharf to the west.

The plots have few prescriptions. There are limitations on height and obligations to building lines – definable courtesies to an evolving urban fabric. But more significant are the expectations and responsibilities in relation to placemaking. The character and context of each space is a major determinant in the planning and architectural outcome of each and every building. Each constructed building reinforces the context for the next. The masterplan,

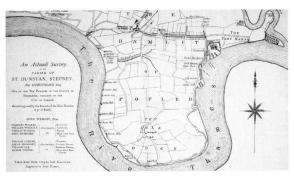

Map of the Isle of Dogs, 1703.

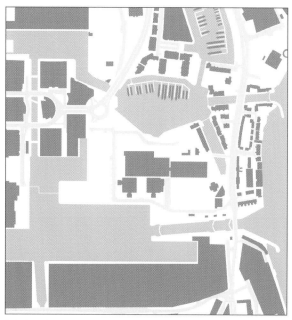
Existing site.

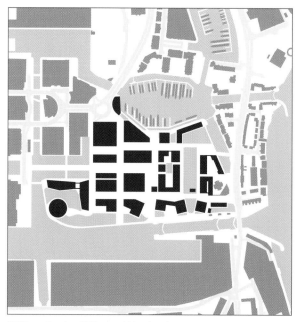
2013 masterplan (Allies and Morrison).

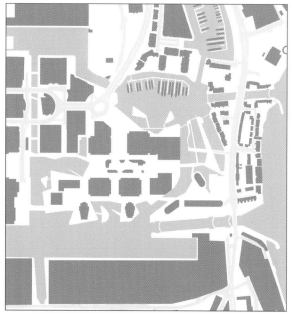
2008 masterplan (Rogers Stirk Harbour + Partners).

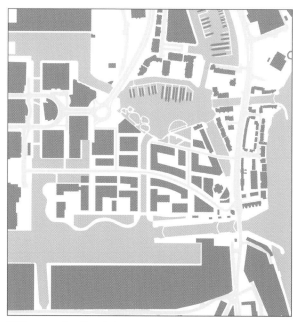
2010 masterplan (Farrells).

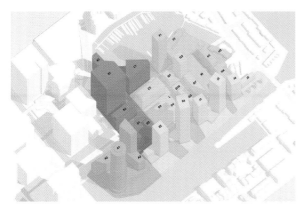

Four distinct quarters, three residential and one commercial, ring a central area.

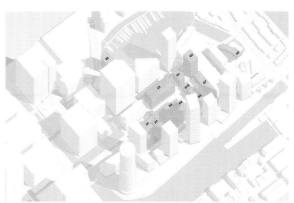

Blocks coloured in green nominated as "swing blocks". They can accommodate a variety of uses.

gradually made manifest, should be as surprising as it is predictable.

When the masterplan is completed, the scale of Wood Wharf may seem compatible with that of Canary Wharf. Its buildings may seem more slender and their disposition more informal – both attributes of a more dominantly residential plan – but the city grid from which they grow will be different. It will encourage a mix of uses. Its spaces will seem more significant than its buildings. And the open weave of its street pattern will connect to the community beyond. It will be joined to Canary Wharf with a causeway but it will also become a part of London's urban fabric.

Above: Physical model of Wood Wharf masterplan. The existing towers of Canary Wharf to the left.

Overleaf: Physical model of ground floor plan of Wood Wharf showing relationship between building interiors and external spaces.

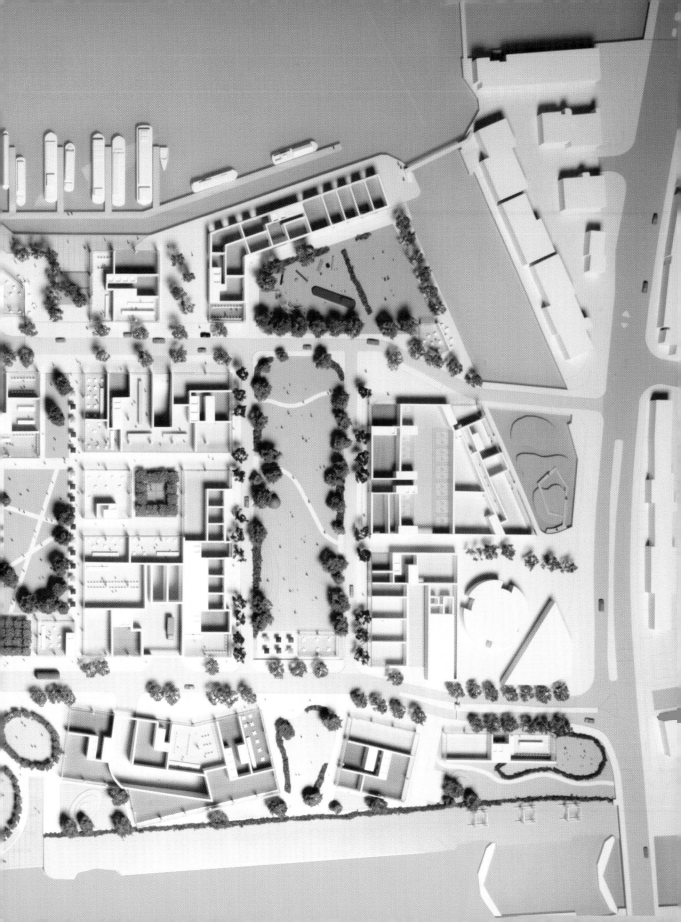

Eminent ground:
tall buildings in the city

Simon Gathercole

The arguments and counter-arguments for the protection or the development of the urban skyline have become a central aspect of the debate regarding the future evolution of our cities. While there are a number of cities in which urban form and tower form have developed a successful symbiotic relationship—New York, Chicago, Hong Kong and Singapore—and there are also instances, as in Yemen, where local vernacular tradition has evolved a fusion between the city block and tower—in contemporary Europe the integration of tall buildings into the streets of our cities remains problematic. The debate in the UK has tended to focus on three issues: on the perceived threat of the tower typology itself, on the impact of towers on the skyline and on the relative merits of different rationales for their location. If one accepts however that tall buildings are inevitable components of our major cities, driven by land values, public transport accessibility and accommodation shortage, what becomes really important is how towers are integrated into the fabric of the city and the quality of the places that they make at street level.

While the processes that define the location of tall buildings at the macro scale are largely out of the hands of architects, the task of embedding these forms into the fabric of the city—its streets, squares and lanes—at the micro scale, falls squarely within the realm of architectural practice, contingent as it is on the scale of the human being, public space and movement.

Just as the architect defines the form, profile, material and detail of the building, determines the organisation of the plan, tests the building for environmental impacts such as wind and overshadowing, so the architect has to take responsibility for integrating the building with the city at its base.

The relationships formed between the building and the public realm—the configuration of the building envelope, the location of entrances and cores, the selection of ground floor uses and the accommodation of service requirements (delivery bays, car park entrances, refuse storage)—are an essential aspect of its integration with the city. The location of the cores, for example, interlocks the vertical figure of the tower to the horizontal patterns of movement and public spaces of the city. In respect of this civic responsibility it is not enough that towers should be shapely and beautifully clad; they must also support the logic of the existing urban fabric and provide relevant ground floor relationships. They should facilitate, rather than frustrate new connections and, when possible, form the edges of public spaces, stimulating and supporting civic life. The way in which these relationships contribute to the quality and coherence of the city now defines the critical territory for the design of tall buildings.

The indisputable prominence that tall buildings enjoy has led many urban commentators to conclude that tall buildings should be treated as landmarks in the city, signifiers of concentrated activity or key locations and to argue that the architecture of towers should be developed accordingly. There is however an alternative position which seeks to draw tall buildings into a closer relationship with the urban fabric of cities and, whilst acknowledging the importance of their visibility from a distance, accepts that at ground level they may benefit from a less assertive approach. What this implies is that tall buildings might assume a more modest role within the city: the idea of a tower as part of a differentiated yet continuous urban fabric rather than as an individual set piece suggests the possibility that tall buildings might be considered as 'background' elements rather than primary figures of the cityscape.

Exactly this approach can be found in many Italian towns and cities. The Romanesque *campanile* of Lucca bristle above the town in brick and stone, dispersed, not clustered, orientating citizens to its various parishes. Narrow converging streets frame the *campanile* of San Frediano set in a small public space behind the *basilica*. The *campanile* of San Marino is embedded in a corner of the Piazza Di San Marino, terraced to one side with the great *duomo* and to the other with secondary buildings that together form the edge of the *piazza*, whilst the Torre Guinigi is differentiated by a rooftop garden of

 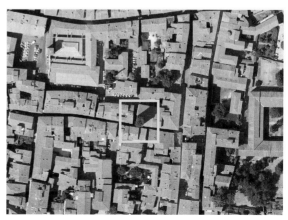

Torre Guinigi, Lucca, fourteenth century.

Campanile Piazza dei Miracoli,
Pisa, twelfth to fourteenth century.

mature oak trees. Each is both a legible, grounded volume and a component of the city fabric, forming the edges of streets and *piazzas*, growing from the everyday bustle of terraced buildings. Whereas in Pisa the famous circular bell tower stands alone, acting, like the baptistery, as a foil to the *duomo*, an isolated statement in a loosely defined open space orientating the people of the city to its religious heart, in Lucca the tower is both subservient to the space it addresses and continuous with the city fabric, pointing to a model for dense urban centres. In contrast, the Pisa model finds its echo in the idea of the 'iconic' tower – the eminence that sets itself apart.

In London the towers of St Mary Axe by Foster + Partners and the Shard by Renzo Piano provide a similar contrast, one a free standing building, circular in plan, standing within a site opened up to receive its idealised form, the other a complex plan shape, continually adjusting as it meets the ground and thereby capable of establishing a relationship with the complex urban fabric – streets, station platforms, railway viaducts – that form its context.

At the Shard two distinct techniques of urban integration are evident. The first is the erosion of the floor-plates to create a transition of form from the base to the top, articulated through the tapering facets which slide past each other to align, define and enclose the public spaces. The second is the use of a mediating building – the Mini Shard – which both establishes a clear relationship with the main tower and shares the scale and typology of the surrounding building context.

The technique of the erosion or the evolution of building floor plates from one level to the next has been explored in a number of contexts. The stepping floor plates of New York skyscrapers enable a densely packed order of tall buildings to coexist. Each undergoes a transition from the discipline of the city block at its base to a proliferation of diverse accommodation above, benefiting from the resultant terraces and balconies as well as the articulation of the facades. More recently the capability to transform

St Mary Axe, City of London (left) and entrance and public realm at the Shard, London (right).

a tall building from one plan shape to another by incrementally adjusting its floor plates has been supported by digital technology and offers alternative possibilities for architects to respond simultaneously to ground level and high level conditions by twisting and tapering the form of the tall building.

The technique of using mediating buildings as part of a masterplan approach to contextualise a tall building is also exemplified by a New York precedent, the Rockefeller Centre. In this case the low rise retail buildings define a series of exceptional public spaces that both set it apart as a civic destination and relate to the scale of 'Old New York', creating a context in which the eminence of the main tower feels appropriate.

Other examples, by contrast, point to a condition where the tall building can be integrated with its context as a background element within a site masterplan or an existing city block. Our student housing scheme on Great Suffolk Street, London, places the tall element at the back of its site, close to a railway viaduct, rather than addressing the street. A terrace building forms the foreground element on the street and completes the perimeter block thereby cutting off lines of sight to the taller element from the immediate public realm. In a similar, earlier, example at One Kemble Street in Covent Garden, Richard Seifert situated a tall cylindrical office building at the corner of two secondary streets off Drury Lane, behind a block that occupies the primary, Kingsway frontage and continues the level of the street frontage established by its nineteenth-century neighbours. In this case the placement of the tower not only allows the urban continuity of Kingsway to be respected but also secures the continuity of the city block, despite the use of the circular plan form.

As cities embark upon a new wave of tall building developments it is essential that we develop a greater understanding of the role that tall buildings play and recognise how their ground floor relationships and the routes and public spaces they create can make more positive, long lasting contributions to an ever more thriving context for city life.

Keybridge House, London.

The strategy for the renewal of the Keybridge House site in Lambeth is guided by its position as a hinge between the proposed tall buildings of the Nine Elms Opportunity Area to the north and the existing mansion blocks to the south. The tall building rises in distinct steps in response to its context – at the fourth floor in relation to the adjacent church, at the eighth floor in relation to the mansion blocks, then at two higher levels to produce a slender profile at the skyline.

Recent tall building proposals by Allies and Morrison showing relationship between building form and ground floor plan.

100 Bishopsgate, City of London.

This corner building in the City of London follows the pre-established street frontage lines at the retail level, with a lozenge shaped, faceted form whose office floor plates are incrementally eroded as it rises through forty-storeys to allow it to evolve into a rectilinear prism, aligned with Bishopsgate. Retail frontages are set back behind a sheltering colonnade and a second office building mediates between the tower and the adjacent nineteenth-century commercial buildings. The project also reinstates an historic back lane beside the Grade I listed St Ethelburga's Church.

Vauxhall Cross, London.

At Vauxhall Cross nine buildings, ranging in height from one to fifty-storeys, cluster around a new public square at the heart of a city block that backs onto the railway viaduct. The slender towers allow space for perimeter buildings that mediate in scale and typology between new and old.

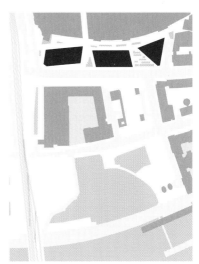

Victoria Street, London.

Adjacent to the entrance to Victoria Station, four new office buildings form a single composition. At their upper levels, these simply-planned efficient buildings reach different heights and stand as individuals. At their lower levels, their truncated pyramidal forms negotiate a transition to a more complex and intricate street pattern at their base.

Eileen House, London.

The parallelogram plan of this residential tower and the triangular shape of the accompanying office building both derive from their site. Together they address the geometry of the adjacent streets and, to the south, form a new public space that collects five separate routes and stands at one end of Keyworth Street – the entrance to South Bank University's main pedestrian spine.

Elizabeth House, London.

The demolition of the existing Elizabeth House office building provides the opportunity to connect Waterloo Station with the River Thames. The two new office buildings signal a new street-level western entrance to the station. This makes a direct connection between the developing South Bank's public realm and each of the station platforms.

Aerial view of Aldgate Place site at the junction of Whitechapel High Street (to north), Leman Street (to west), and Commercial Road (to south-west).

Aldgate Place

London

Three residential towers containing four hundred and sixty three new homes, together with a one hundred and fifty-bed hotel, are inserted into a key urban site on the edge of the City of London.

Fundamental to our approach to urbanism is a conviction that when new buildings, or new groups of buildings, or new urban plans, are introduced into the body of the city, their first obligation is to achieve an appropriate level of integration with their immediate context, to support and reinforce the urban matrix of which they form a part. What this implies is a certain mistrust of projects which are too self-referential or inward-looking, projects conceived as self-contained, set-pieces, more concerned with their own inner logic than with the workings of the world around them.

It is true however that there are examples, in London and elsewhere, of urban set-pieces that do succeed in both standing out and fitting in, projects that are able, through their careful combination of complementary buildings and spaces, to project their own discrete identity at the same time as they support the continuity of the city that surrounds them.

London's earliest example, probably, is Covent Garden, a space which is now dominated by the nineteenth-century market building but which was originally characterised by the elegant brick facades of the housing that enclosed it on three sides and the rhetorical portico of St Paul's Church which formed its eastern edge. Later examples include, famously, John Nash's Regent Street. But there are also many less familiar examples such as the crescent of the Aldwych, the mansion blocks to the east of the Royal Albert Hall, or Sicilian Avenue, the small street of shops that provides a satisfying short-cut between Southampton Row and Bloomsbury Way. Our proposals for Aldgate Place follow in this tradition.

The history of the Aldgate Place site is a curious one. Although outside the Aldgate, and therefore beyond the boundary of both the Roman and the medieval city, the area had nevertheless established by the end of the eighteenth century a strong urban grid, with a pattern of east–west and north–south streets that followed the alignment of Whitechapel High Street, the original Roman road linking London to Colchester.

At the beginning of the nineteenth century however, this simple urban pattern was subverted by the introduction of the diagonal of Commercial Road, a major new thoroughfare cut through the existing urban fabric by the East India Company in order to allow this immensely influential organisation to connect its newly constructed docks more directly back into the City.

This new diagonal configuration survived into the first half of the twentieth century, and for many years the junction of Commercial Road with Whitechapel High Street was known by the name of the department store that occupied one of the rather awkward triangular sites that resulted: Gardiner's Corner.

The destruction of Gardiner's Corner in a bombing raid during the Second World War allowed the diagonal configuration to be supplanted by a new road pattern, one

Map of site, 1799.

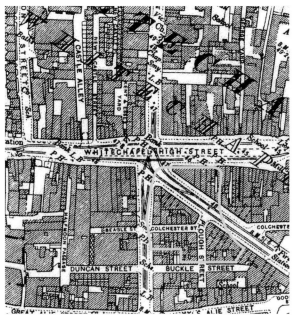

Map of site, 1891.

Gardiner's Corner, 1930s.

of a series of large-scale gyratory systems that were instigated in London during the post-war years to accelerate the flow of traffic at what were identified as particularly critical junctions.

What resulted, in urban terms, from this piece of traffic planning was never satisfactory – for the pedestrian it created a hostile environment that was enormously difficult to use – and in recent years the gyratory was itself removed. A new, simpler, highway configuration was introduced allowing a new public landscape to be created on the site of one of the redundant roads – Braham Street – and providing an opportunity to establish a new urban structure on the Aldgate Place site, the primary challenge of this project.

While this might suggest the possibility of restoring the original orthogonal street pattern, the reality is that the complex history of the site cannot, even if it was desirable, be so easily wiped away. The historical route defined by Drum Street/Commercial Road contains below its surface a vast array of utilities – pipes, cables, wires – which are prohibitively expensive to remove. The only possibility today is to preserve them in situ and arrange the new

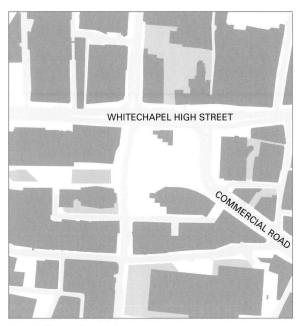

Aldgate Place: urban fabric as existing.

Aldgate Place: urban fabric as proposed.

accommodation in such a way that all the various services can remain fully accessible for inspection and maintenance in the future.

The search for a new urban pattern for the site capable of both accommodating, easily and naturally, the Drum Street diagonal, and integrating the development back into the pre-existing street pattern, led to a proposal for three triangular or, more accurately, kite-shaped towers. Because of their plan configuration, these towers – together with the three lower structures that extend from them at their base – have the capacity not only to relate to, and define, the diagonal of Drum Street, but also, critically, to re-establish the continuity of the building lines on Leman Street, Whitechapel High Street, Buckle Street and Commercial Road. Just as importantly because of its acute corners the kite-shape plan produces a high proportion of dual-aspect flats.

While the three towers all share a common plan configuration, the three lower buildings that abut them each adopt a different form, in response partly to the

differences in the uses they contain, and partly to the role they play within the site, assimilating the new development into the pre-existing context. The building in the north-east corner is an office building with higher floor to floor heights and a unique pattern of fenestration. The building in the south-east corner contains a second core and forms the connection with the lower buildings of Commercial Road. And the building on the south-west corner is entirely residential and faces out across Braham Street Park.

The roofs of each of the lower buildings also provide locations for external amenity spaces – gardens – related to each of the towers. One of the challenges of building housing at this density, even when a minority of the units will be occupied by families, is to create sufficient opportunities for informal play and recreation. So the use of the roof in this way is important, as is that of the public landscape at ground floor levels and the community space included at the base of one of the buildings.

In the centre of the site, in a space defined by the flanks of each of the three towers and set apart from any of the

other buildings, stands the hotel, a nine-storey building with public facilities on the lower two floors and a reception room and garden on the roof. Configuring the hotel in this way, as an entirely freestanding building, has made it possible to encircle it with a continuous network of public routes, one of which is treated as a small enclosed garden. It is imagined that the garden would operate much like the small churchyards found across the city, shut at night, but fully open to the public from dawn to dusk.

Of the masterplans contained within this book, Aldgate Place is one of the densest, at six hundred and ninety one dwellings per hectare. This is new territory for London, but territory that will become more familiar as we seek to accommodate more people using less land in all our urban centres.

Opposite: Perspective of new pedestrian space following the original alignment of Commercial Road.

Diagrams showing evolution of plan.

Early study model establishing the principle of three kite-shaped residential towers.

Physical model of the current scheme.

Reappraising the mansion block: density as a typological trigger

Alfredo Caraballo

London today is experiencing a period of substantial change, one that is radically altering the identity of the city, both in terms of its density and its scale. The exponential demand for residential units is unlikely to be achieved using low rise typologies alone. Famous as a city formed from rows of terraced houses, London is changing into one made of apartment blocks and towers. This increase in density can be seen as part of a new chapter in London's history, and with it comes an obligation to consider the type of city we want to build and the typologies that will facilitate this.

London has gone through several such changes in the past. The economic growth associated with the industrial revolution in the nineteenth century generated unprecedented increases in density, and at both ends of the social structure new typologies were conceived to enable more people to live together more tightly. On one hand new forms of social housing were proposed by benefactors like Guinness and Peabody to address the appalling conditions of the working class population. On the other, new types of 'palaces' for the wealthy classes were proposed to address the need to create taller and denser types of residential buildings. In both cases, one typology dominated: the mansion block.

The mansion block first appeared in London in the second half of the nineteenth century following developments in continental Europe, particularly in France. It offered a response not only to issues of density and of how to build vertically but also, crucially, to the matter of urban decorum. If it was no longer possible – because of rising land costs – for the wealthy to build individual 'houses', under what circumstances might they be able to share the same plot, the same stairs, the same address in a 'dignified' manner? At the same time, but at the other end of the social spectrum, concern was growing as to how to improve mass housing for the working classes. Although each mansion block is different and unique, certain common traits can be traced relating to the organisation of their plans, the articulation of their elevations and their manipulation of ornament.

The mansion block fulfils the pragmatic need for the repetition of apartments, but represents this repetition externally with the architecture of the palace. There is a conscious, and necessarily relaxed, disjunction between the appearance of the building and its internal logic: the former deals with the obligations of the building to the city and with issues of urban decorum while the latter deals with the particularities of the internal layout. As a result, behind rich and elaborated elevations we often find rational and straightforward plans.

rt·Hall·Mansions·South·Kensington·
· R·Norman·Shaw·R·A·Architect·

Albert Hall Mansions, South
Kensington, London; R Norman
Shaw, 1880–87.

The mansion block: ornament and inhabitation.

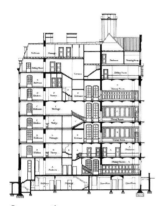

Cross-section
of Albert Hall Mansions.

The notion of a 'palace', or grand mansion, implies a sense of unity and independence while their inherent scale gives them an urban status and presence on the street beyond that of the individual or terraced house. The expression of the building as a whole – often a substantial, singular structure – is counter-balanced by the rich detailing and elaboration of its facades.

While the attraction of the mansion block for the commercial speculator or the social philanthropist lay in its regularity and efficiency, its repetitive floor plans were often concealed by carefully elaborated facades and highly articulated massing. An often delicate balance was sought between the repetitive elements of the composition of a block and the incidental accents that articulate each elevation. Efficiency might have dictated that the living rooms or service areas would be in the same location on each floor, but this did not imply that any one window should look the same as the one on the floor below.

The elevation of a mansion block is rarely a flat surface. A detailed wall section can reveal a complex system of recesses and projections of windows, cornices, cills, balconies. These elements articulate the composition of each elevation. In contrast, the rear elevations are often repetitive and plain.

If its front wall is a complex, layered surface, the profile of the mansion block is typically elaborated to produce a distinctive skyline. A profusion of essentially straightforward elements – mansard roofs, chimneys, party walls, skylights – are treated as a compositional system. While this approach may have had it roots in the theories of the Gothic Revival and the Arts and Crafts, it soon evolved into a set of architectural themes which became the trademark of the mansion block: elaborated corners, recessed roofs, oversized dormers, even small pavilions on the roof.

The articulation of the elevations of mansion blocks – their massing and profile – is underpinned by a picturesque sensibility, a response to the role the buildings play within the city. Ornament and embellishment are deliberately employed as a gesture to the public realm. Like wearing one's best clothes in public, it is a matter of propriety. Front elevations are rich and layered. The base of the building is articulated and acknowledges the passers-by. Entrances are highlighted, and thresholds clearly identified. Ornament is used as a natural and conventional tool.

Unsurprisingly, modernism reacted strongly against the elaborate system of conventions and styles that flourished at the end of the nineteenth century. Today it seems possible to look again at these typologies without the burden of ideology or aesthetic prejudices. What was once seen as a problematic and decadent form of housing might in fact inform progressive, new solutions. And the mansion flat typology, developed in response to a previous substantial change in the notion of the city, might once again offer useful clues to the design of urban housing.

The redundant Keybridge House.

Keybridge

London

This proposal to introduce four hundred and fifteen dwellings on the site of a redundant telecoms switching station, built in the 1970s, explores how different residential typologies might be brought together into a single 'ensemble' in which each component plays a particular role in relation to the historic, current and emerging context of the site.

As might be anticipated from its location – next to the Vauxhall Nine Elms Opportunity Area with its new tall buildings cluster on one side and within the Vauxhall Conservation Area on the other – the site has to address very different conditions: a busy main road as well as quieter residential streets; a large park, as well as a railway viaduct; small scale Victorian buildings, as well as a cluster of new towers now proposed within the Opportunity Area.

The aim of the project is to make a specific, discrete response to each of its three street edges. On Wyvil Road, a low, linear, residential building redefines the street

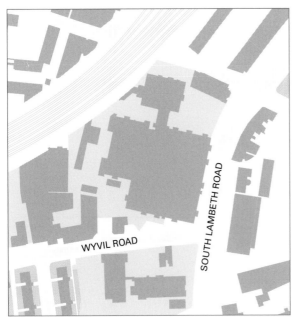

Keybridge: urban fabric as existing.

Keybridge: urban fabric as proposed.

frontage and re-engages with the existing Victorian public house that stands on the street corner. Beyond the pub, a new primary school completes the street and provides an end stop to Trenchold Street.

The scale and character of South Lambeth Road demands a different approach. Here we have acknowledged the relevance of existing precedents like the near-by Victoria Mansion and Park Mansions, but also some of the now demolished mansion blocks that previously lined the street. Because of their scale, as well as their articulation and elaboration, the typology of the mansion block seems particularly appropriate to the context of the conservation area. The formality of their front facades helps to define a strong street edge whereas the informality of their 'backs' allows a different relationship to be established with the new houses through the further articulation of the massing. Two new mansion blocks are proposed on South Lambeth Road restoring the scale and materiality that characterised the street in the past, while introducing new shop fronts to animate their base.

Two tall buildings play a significant role in the composition. In part they constitute a response to the scale of the emerging context of the Vauxhall Nine Elms cluster of tall buildings on the other side of the railway viaduct, but in their form and appearance they are also intended to relate to the architectural character of the rest of the project. Constructed from a robust and pared down language of brick – reflecting the local, industrial vernacular – they also enjoy a degree of articulation that allows them to be sympathetic to the mansion blocks and other buildings in the vicinity. The towers are neither simple extrusions of a form in plan nor an over-elaborate shape; they are instead stepped forms that fold and adjust in response to the emerging and existing wider context through their silhouette and mass.

The new spaces formed between the buildings change in character through their location on the site with a variety of public, shared and private spaces including mews paved with brick setts as well as lush planted courtyards incorporating amenity and play space.

Aerial view of St Andrews, Bow site showing configuration of redundant
hospital building and relationship to the A12 urban motorway.

St Andrews, Bromley-by-Bow

London

A residential masterplan provides for the replacement
of a redundant hospital with a matrix of new streets and
public spaces.

St Andrews, the nineteenth-century hospital that formerly occupied this site, functioned as an enclosed precinct physically separated from the city that surrounded it. In contrast, this masterplan for nine hundred and sixty four new dwellings on a 3 hectare site proposed an open-grained structure of streets and blocks, intended to promote movement into and across the site and integrate the new development back into the fabric of the surrounding area.

A simple pattern of long courtyard buildings establishes a clear urban matrix within the site and re-establishes strong street frontages to its west and south. Aligned on a north-south axis in order to maximise the number of east and

west facing flats, the blocks are also lower on their south side to allow more sunlight into the courtyard gardens.

The informal geometry of the buildings changes the character of both the courtyard spaces and the intermediate streets, emphasising, paradoxically, the sense of openness of the courtyards and the sense of enclosure of the streets. The streets, while capable of carrying traffic, prioritise the busy domestic life of the buildings on either side, effectively acting as 'home zones'.

The eastern edge of the site presented a more unusual challenge with the need to reconcile a certain defensiveness in response to the hostile environment of the multi-level

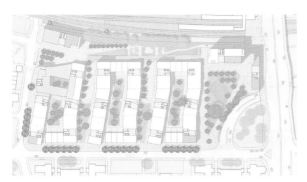

Site plan showing configuration of the new street blocks and arrangement of courtyards.

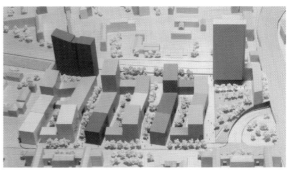

Model illustrating the masterplan principle of the courtyard blocks being composed of separate, but linked, buildings.

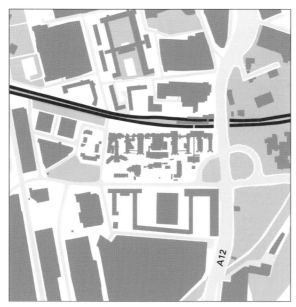

St Andrews, Bromley-by-Bow: urban fabric as existing.

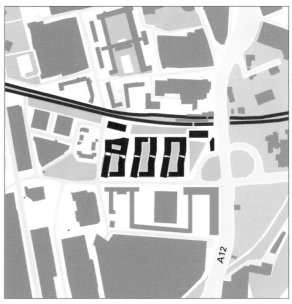

St Andrews, Bromley-by-Bow: urban fabric as proposed.

A12 road junction with an obligation to forge as strong and as attractive a connection as possible to Bromley-by-Bow underground station, the entrance to which is located on the edge of the dual carriageway.

In the past developments along this busy road have typically turned their back on its noisy and rather threatening environment. It is the sort of response which we regard, however, as counterproductive, as it only reinforces the negative qualities of the prevailing urban environment.

Our masterplan therefore took a more positive approach, concentrating the majority of the public green space that our scheme would generate into this position. The resulting new park improves the route to and from the station for everybody within the local area and provides a visual buffer between the new buildings and the road. A small community building built on a prominent site next to the road also provides some further protection.

In addition to the linear blocks, the masterplan provided the location for two residential towers one on the north-west and one on the north-east corner where their height would not cause overshadowing.

It was always the intention that individual buildings within the development would be designed by different architects and a set of design guidelines were prepared balancing diversity with unity. All the lower buildings have projecting balconies, profiled rooflines and front doors onto the street. And all the buildings are faced in brick.

Bottom left: Cross-section through the courtyard showing the ground floor and top floor duplex family units.

Opposite: View of communal courtyard gardens.

Entrance to the courtyard.

New street frontage, Devas Street.

Facade to the garden.

Entrance on the street.

Public art installation at the entrance to the garden designed by Bobby Lloyd.

Overleaf: Individual front doors to the ground floor family dwellings.

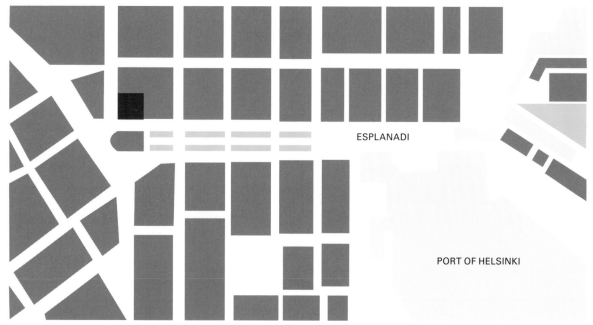

ESPLANADI

PORT OF HELSINKI

Plan of Central Helsinki showing position of the
Academic Bookstore in the city's urban hierarchy.

**Making sense of the city:
Stockmann's Academic Bookstore**

Stockmann's Academic Bookstore, Alvar Aalto, 1969.

Designed by Alvar Aalto in 1969, Stockmann's Academic Bookstore occupies a corner site in the centre of Helsinki at the junction of Pohjoisesplandi and Keskuskatu. Although both facades of the building were clad in the same bronze curtain wall, the significance of the major street – the Esplanade – was acknowledged by Aalto through the addition of a white marble lining to the window reveals. In this way the city's urban hierarchy is made explicit, and the building is assimilated naturally within it.

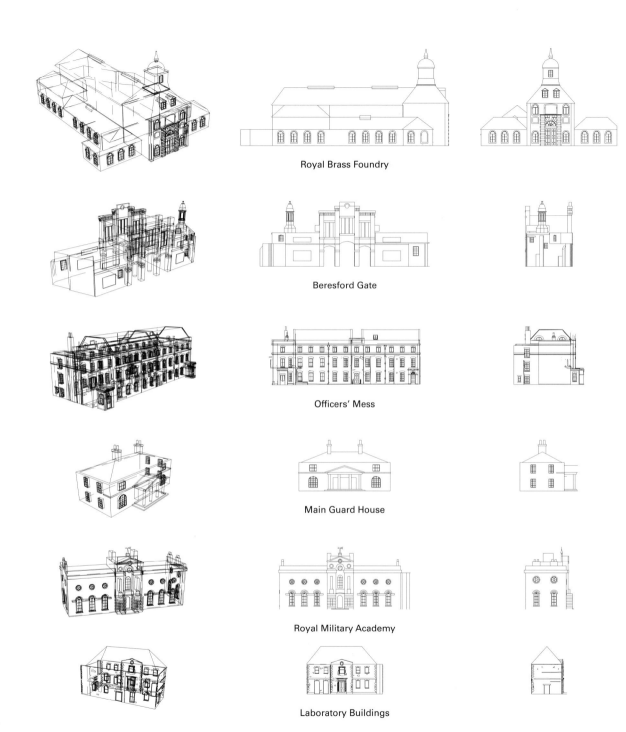

Royal Brass Foundry

Beresford Gate

Officers' Mess

Main Guard House

Royal Military Academy

Laboratory Buildings

Drawings of some of the historic buildings of Woolwich Arsenal
retained and revealed as part of the masterplan.

Royal Arsenal Woolwich

London

The centre of Woolwich is undergoing a period of significant change following the decision to provide the town with both a Crossrail and a Docklands Light Railway station. Of all the new investments, in the town centre, the largest is at the Royal Arsenal where more than five thousand dwellings are being created.

While the origins of the Royal Arsenal at Woolwich lie as far back as the sixteenth century, and some of its most important buildings date from the late seventeenth and early eighteenth centuries, the peak of its operation as a vast military industrial site occurred just before the First World War when the land it occupied extended over 485 hectares and it employed a workforce of eighty thousand people.

During the Second World War its vulnerability to enemy air attack led Churchill to disperse its functions to different sites across the country, a decision that precipitated its gradual decline. By 1967 the production of ordnance had ceased entirely and the site was finally closed in 1994, a huge if unavoidable loss to the local economy.

Ownership of the land around the buildings – a tantalising combination of distinguished architectural set-pieces and substantial, workaday, Victorian structures – passed to a succession of public bodies before eventually being transferred to the London Development Agency. The LDA recognised its potential as an engine for the renewal of the whole of Woolwich town centre, and secured the involvement of Berkeley Homes in its development.

But what really transformed the potential of the site were two far-reaching transport initiatives. The first is the extension of the Docklands Light Railway, which placed Woolwich within two stops of City Airport and twenty five minutes from the new financial centre of Canary Wharf. And the second – taken seven years later – was the

Aerial view of the site with Woolwich town centre in the foreground and the River Thames and the Royal Docks to the north.

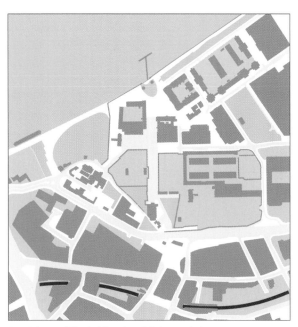

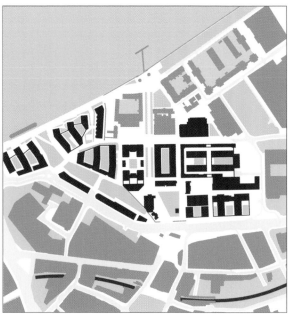

Royal Arsenal Woolwich: urban fabric as existing.

Royal Arsenal Woolwich: urban fabric as proposed.

reconfiguration of the southern Crossrail route to include a station at Woolwich, the funding for which would be largely provided for by the new development.

The result was a place in which it became more attractive to live, and therefore a more attractive site in which to invest, but also one for which a much higher density of development was justified. From being perceived as a marginal site on the edge of London in an area of significant deprivation, the Arsenal began to be seen as an opportunity to create a major, new urban quarter.

Our role as masterplanner did not commence until 2005 at a point when the first phases of development – focussed on the restoration and conversion of the existing buildings and the paving of Number One Street – were already underway.

The next task was to set out a pattern for development on the cleared areas of the site that would enable new buildings to be introduced without compromising the setting of the historic structures or sacrificing the unique atmosphere of the site.

Three successive versions of the masterplan were prepared, as the brief for the site – in particular the requirements for Crossrail – continued to evolve. But the principles of the masterplan have always remained the same.

In the historic part of the site – in the area defined by the enclosure of the original boundary wall – the character and disposition of the new buildings is related directly to the form and identity of the old. All the new buildings conform to the same simple orthogonal grid that had previously shaped the eighteenth and nineteenth-century plan of the site, while allowing a finer grain of pedestrian routes to percolate through it. The smaller brick buildings have been preserved and provided with a new context that will allow them to participate beneficially in the new development, sometimes opening out onto the new public spaces (Dial Arch Square), sometimes defining areas of open space (Laboratory Buildings) and sometimes forming the perimeter to larger development parcels (Building Ten).

The heights of the new buildings in this area of the site are generally also constrained by the maximum heights of the

Physical model of second stage of the masterplan showing new
linear park connecting the town centre to the river.

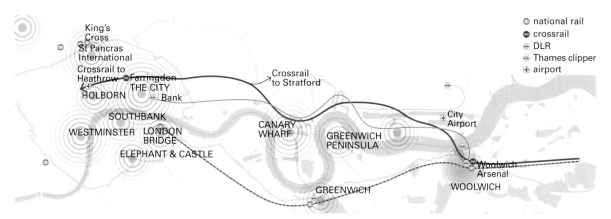

⊖ national rail
⊖ crossrail
⊖ DLR
⊖ Thames clipper
⊕ airport

King's
Cross
St Pancras
International
Crossrail to
Heathrow ⊖Farringdon
HOLBORN THE CITY
⊖ Bank
Crossrail
to Stratford
SOUTHBANK
WESTMINSTER LONDON
BRIDGE
CANARY
WHARF
GREENWICH
PENINSULA
City
Airport
ELEPHANT & CASTLE
Woolwich
Arsenal
WOOLWICH
GREENWICH

Map showing how the new transport infrastructure of the
Docklands Light Railway and Crossrail will supplement existing
rail connection to central London.

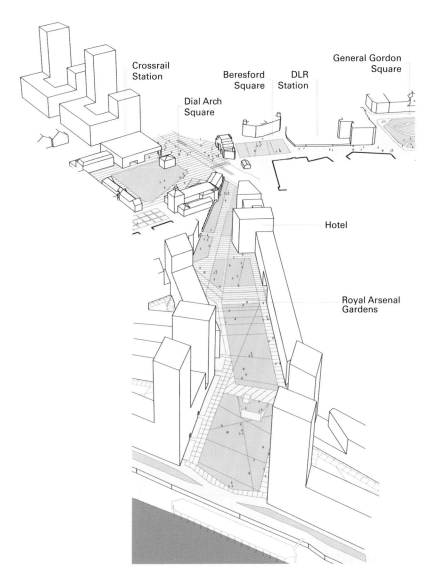

Crossrail
Station

Beresford
Square

DLR
Station

General Gordon
Square

Dial Arch
Square

Hotel

Royal Arsenal
Gardens

existing building with taller buildings only being permitted on the southern boundary on Plumstead Road, next to the town centre and above the new Crossrail station. The entrance to the station itself is located in Dial Arch Square, helping to ensure that the historic space is enjoyed by all the residents of Woolwich and not just the residents of the Arsenal.

Where the new development is situated outside the historic site – in the area known as the Warren – a new park links the town centre directly to the river, part of a chain of new public spaces that descend through the centre of Woolwich including General Gordon Square and Beresford Square.

The setting out of new buildings and spaces in The Warren addresses a series of external geometries, including the alignment of Plumstead Road, the location of the Crossrail tunnel and the river itself.

In the interior of the site similar courtyard typologies have been used as those employed within the Arsenal proper, but on the river frontage taller, freestanding, linear buildings have been introduced to take advantage of the openness of this position.

Above: Constructed on the line of the Crossrail tunnel, the new park connects the town centre to the river.

Opposite: Sketch view looking north towards the river.

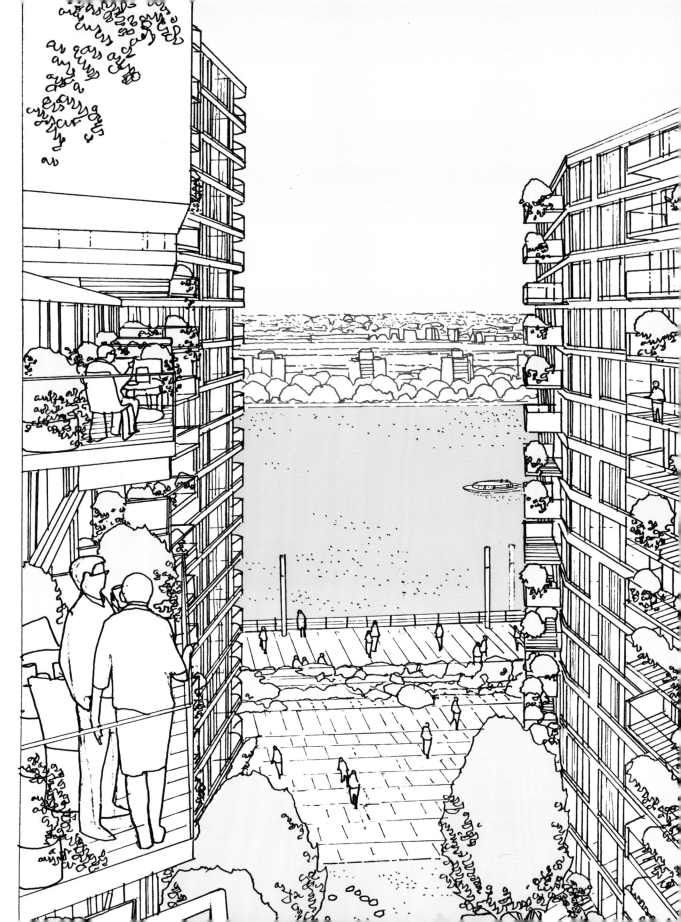

Looking south up Number One Street towards the Royal Brass Foundry and Woolwich town centre.

New residential buildings integrated into the historic fabric.

Dial Arch Square with the first of the new residential buildings behind.

Royal Military Academy and Parade Ground.

What a masterplan does (and what it doesn't)

Bob Allies

A masterplan has two functions.

Firstly it has to set out a vision for the future of a site that will not only inspire and guide the development process, but will also elicit, in advance of any detailed architectural proposals, the support – and therefore the approval – of the various public authorities whose responsibility it is to oversee it.

Secondly, it has to provide a template for the development that is sufficiently clear and sufficiently reliable – and, indeed, that has been sufficiently tested – to allow the decision to be taken to implement the project by those who carry the financial responsibility for its realisation.

In order to achieve these two objectives a masterplan must present a clear understanding of the type of place, or places, it will create: the scale and character of the buildings, the function and configuration of the public spaces, the extent and distribution of the anticipated uses. This is necessary in order to provide reassurance for client, planners, and public alike as to the quality of the urban environment that will result. Just as importantly, it will enable reliable assessments to be made as to the quantum of the accommodation that it will produce – or the value that it will generate – and therefore of the level of investment that can be justified. It should go without saying that the plan must also define rationally sized and shaped development parcels that will prove capable of producing the quantum, and the quality, of the accommodation that has been promised. In this regard, it seems logical that parcels that are unduly compromised by geometric idiosyncrasies or formal obligations should generally be avoided.

In parallel with this pursuit of its own internal logic, a masterplan also has a duty to engage with its wider context – to make new connections into and across the site, to adjust to the scale and character of the adjacent neighbourhoods, and to compensate for deficiencies in the existing social infrastructure and open space provision. At its simplest it has, in other words, an obligation to integrate itself into its immediate neighbourhood. But at its best, it offers an opportunity to stimulate and to contribute to the area's wider regeneration.

A truly successful masterplan, as well as being concerned with the nature of the product, must also consider the nature of the process. It is so obvious a point that it seems absurd to have to make it, but the fundamental purpose of a masterplan is to facilitate development, not inhibit it. This is, however, something which many masterplans fail either to understand or to acknowledge. A masterplan which is over-complex, which, for example, relies upon a singular, all-embracing geometry or requires excessive up-front infrastructure investment is more likely to prevent the commencement of a project than precipitate it. Put simply, the design of a masterplan should make it easy for those intending to carry it out to make the first move, to lay the first foundation, something which it can do best by providing confidence in the long-term viability – and flexibility – of the project.

In recent years there have been a plethora of masterplans which rely for their authority on the incorporation of highly particular and rigorously prescriptive geometries, plans which require all their constituent parts to conform to the overriding formal predilections of the masterplanner: radiating patterns, serpentine lines, circular footprints, rhomboidal plans. Such propositions are no different to the Beaux-Arts plans of the nineteenth century and equally anachronistic. An urban plan is not a graphic pattern, it is a definition of future relationships. What a masterplan does is describe an urban hierarchy, a hierarchy that is both sufficiently clear that it can allow the first building to be constructed – the first move to take place – and sufficiently practical that it can guide the subsequent implementation of the project. The task of the urban designer is not to create attractive shapes and patterns, however engaging they are to the author or seductive they are for the client.

A process, not a product

Where the sorts of plans described above particularly fail is in their ability to assimilate change within the lifetime of the project. Large-scale masterplans take many years to implement. So a plan which imposes an exaggerated, and highly personal, formal discipline on the ensuing development will almost certainly be enormously difficult to carry out. Taking the decision to embark on a project of this scale is extraordinarily hard when you know that your first move, in one corner of the site, will define what your last move will have to be, in the opposite corner, some twenty five years later. Rather, what is needed is a plan that while offering sufficient certainty at the outset of the project also embodies sufficient flexibility to evolve and change in the course of its implementation. A masterplan is a process, not a product.

This has led us in our masterplans to resist the introduction of any kind of singular, overbearing, geometric determinacy and instead adopt a certain informality, a degree of open-endedness. We avoid the imposition of arbitrary sequences and shapes at the outset of a project as, indeed, we resist overly prescriptive physical codes during its implementation. Such measures, we believe, only constrain or compromise future architectural expression. Instead we seek forms of order which can welcome and absorb a variety of individual design responses, collages, rather than patterns.

A masterplan is not a building

The point is a simple one. Designing a masterplan is not the same as designing a building. For an architect to require all the elements of a building to conform to a single, all-embracing geometry is both logical and desirable. A masterplan, however, is realised through the combined efforts of many people over a long period of time. For an urban designer to impose a single aesthetic vision throughout this extended process would be highly problematic. Each architect at every stage would have to embrace the eccentricity of each curiously shaped site, and each building would have to participate in an unusually intimate and specific way with each of its neighbours. This would constitute an aesthetic constraint that few designers would find engaging. To attempt to make a city in this way would surely prove impossible.

What a good masterplan does need to provide is sufficient certainty in the nature of the urban fabric it proposes so that individual buildings can be brought forward confident in the role they play within that fabric. In this regard, what the masterplan offers – in the absence of an established context for the building – is, in effect, a surrogate context, a clearly understood framework within which individual buildings can be designed and against which they can be assessed. At the same time, it is also critically important that sufficient flexibility is included within the description of the masterplan to allow its continuing evolution in response to the sorts of changes in demand and expectation that will inevitably emerge in the course of the implementation process.

When we develop a masterplan, we therefore work within what are, effectively, a set of self-imposed rules. These rules are not aesthetic but practical, and they relate to our understanding of how to ensure that the masterplan will, over time, prove to be as useful and as productive as possible.

What are these rules?

Firstly, for the reasons set out above, we avoid the temptation to design the masterplan as if it were a building. That is to say, we resist imposing any form of site-wide ordering device – either conceptual or geometric – to which everything is required to conform. Such an approach is, we believe, neither helpful at the start of the project – when it suggests commitments that subsequent stages may not be able to honour – nor during its implementation, when it inevitably reduces flexibility and limits options.

Secondly, we search always for an urban structure that has a clear and comprehensible hierarchy, one with which individual buildings, as they are brought forward, can straightforwardly and sympathetically, comply. We think it is important, in other words, that, for example, the masterplan is clear as to where is the front and where is the back of a building, and that individual buildings should be designed to reflect the differences in these two conditions.

Thirdly and lastly, we resist the development of any kind of synthetic solution in which a series of buildings share a common infrastructure. Cities are dynamic organisms, and individual buildings within a masterplan should be capable at any point of being demolished and replaced by something new. Anything that makes this too difficult should therefore be avoided.

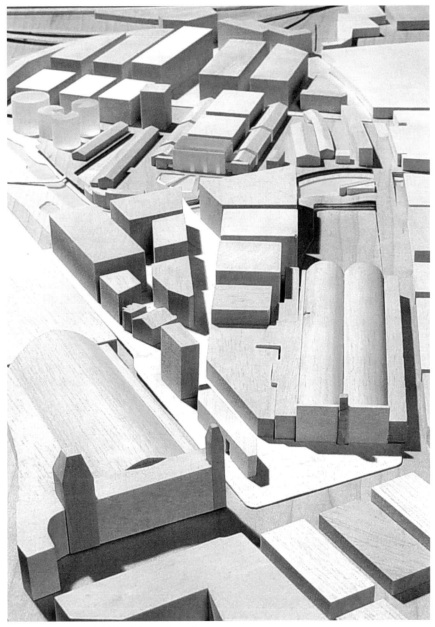

Timber concept model, King's Cross Central.

Looking north up the valley of the River Lea from the Thames to
the Olympics site.

Olympic Games and Legacy

Lea Valley, London

The task of the masterplan for the London 2012 Olympic and Paralympic Games was not just to facilitate the event itself, but also to ensure that as much as possible of the huge financial investment in the Games would benefit the present and future residents of what was previously one of the most deprived areas of London.

At the heart of the London Olympic masterplan was a very simple diagram. In the centre of the site was a wide public concourse. This was surrounded by a ring of venues: the stadium, the aquatics centre, the velodrome, as well as arenas for hockey, handball, water polo and basketball. Around these were all the temporary structures that fed and supported the Games. The pattern was similar to that of Beijing but the London concourse was substantially smaller: the venues in London were clustered more closely together, around a public space that was much reduced in size. This reflected one of the underlying principles of

the London Olympics: restrict what is built for the Games to that which is actually required. It is an approach that seems likely to be repeated elsewhere in the future as the scope and scale of the Games – what must be delivered to make it happen and how much money is spent in the process – comes under increasing scrutiny.

But what was of even greater importance in shaping the plan of the London Games was a determination that the substantial financial outlay necessary for the Olympics – and it is still a colossal investment that has been made into the site – would deliver a legacy that would go beyond

Before the games, the site consisted of a combination of low-grade industrial uses and pockets of natural landscape.

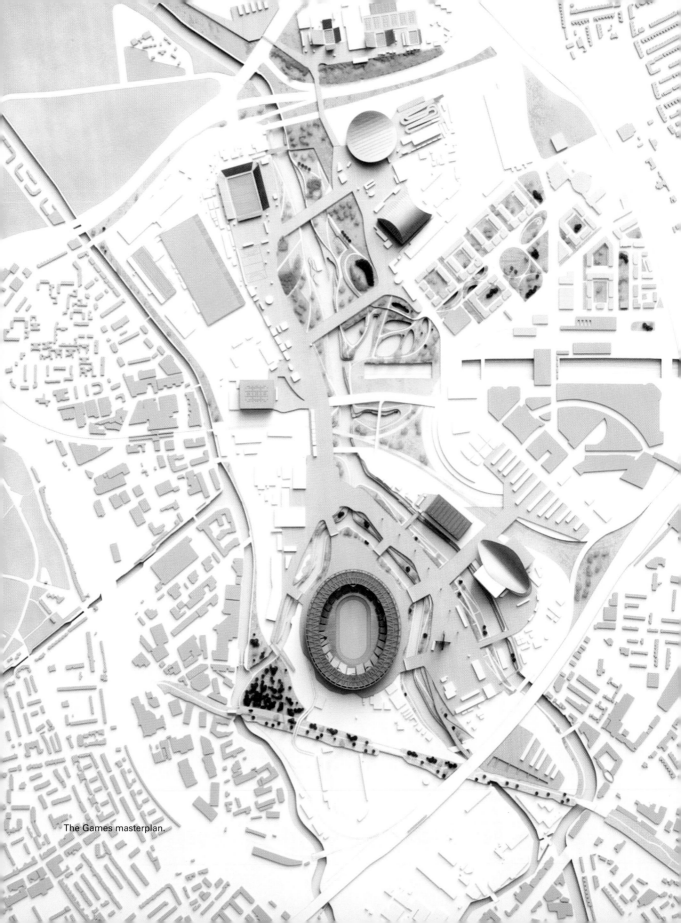

The Games masterplan.

The Games masterplan established a clear distinction between a lower level – that of the river valley – and an upper level, where the Olympic concourse was located. This meant that the implementation of the valley landscape could proceed early while the detailed design of the concourse and the venues were still being developed. Post-games the lower level has been retained largely unchanged while the upper level has been reclaimed as parkland, an informal open landscape in the north and a more intense, metropolitan park in the south.

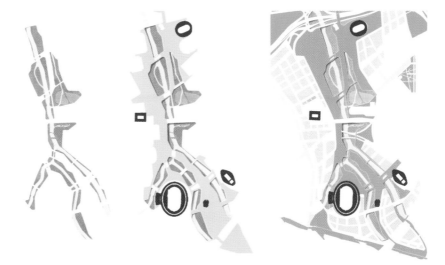

the individual amenities inherited from the Games – the park and the venues – to create enduring benefits for the whole of the area of east London in which it is set. In fact the site for the Olympics falls within the curtilage of four separate London boroughs namely Newham, Tower Hamlets, Hackney and Waltham Forest, four boroughs which are among the most deprived within the capital. So the arrival, courtesy of the Olympics, of an investment of this magnitude, and within such a compressed time scale, was clearly an event of extraordinary local significance.

Not that the area was entirely devoid of development in the years leading up to the Games. New proposals were coming forward, new buildings were being built. But everything that was happening was happening in an essentially pragmatic and ad hoc way. The Olympics provided an opportunity to take a far more radical and comprehensive approach to the transformation of the area, allowing a single, coordinated plan for the Lea Valley to be prepared that could exploit the various improvements to infrastructure – for example, the undergrounding of the electricity cables –

The Olympic park forms a vital link in a planned green route extending from the outside of London to its centre.

Informal planting leading down to the river.

Bridge abutment and balustrade. Gabions
filled with recycled material from the site.

Approach to the stadium from Stratford City.　　New road bridge, Ruckholt Road.

The Legacy masterplan.

Sketches illustrating differences in urban character across the site.

which the Games would require, and which without the Games, simply would not have happened.

The aim, then, of the Legacy masterplan was to use the investment of the Games to set in motion the creation of a new piece of city. Up to thirty thousand residents will be accommodated in a series of five neighbourhoods that bridge between the landscape of the Olympic Park and the adjacent pre-existing communities on either side of the valley. Depending on its location within the overall site, the nature of the housing will vary from relatively small scale – two, three and four-storey houses, modelled on London's historical residential typologies – to larger scale, higher density urban blocks in areas adjacent to public transport nodes. In each location, the Legacy plan provides detailed design guidance in order to characterise the nature of the development that will follow and ensure its contribution to the wider setting, the rivers, roads and parklands that thread their way through the site.

The location identified for the Games was a 240 hectare site in the valley of the River Lea, an area of land previously in industrial use. In fact, the River Lea – a tributary of the Thames – has always created a divide within London, a line of separation between the body of the city and its eastern extension. The reason for this is that the quality of the land in the valley – low-lying, marshy and liable to flood – always rendered it both hazardous to cross and difficult to build on. It was for this reason, too, that historically the valley increasingly became the location for so many of the messy, but essential, back-of-house functions that a city like London has to accommodate. In effect, the Lea Valley acted as London's back yard, with depots for buses, stabling for underground trains, sewage treatment works, gasworks, power generation and transmission, railway sidings, warehousing, goods distribution, urban motorways, waste storage and waste treatment all finding a home here. Indeed the finest

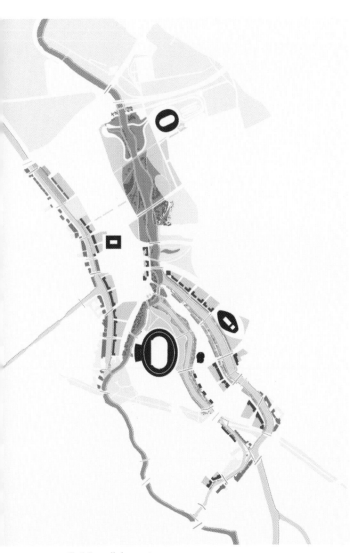

Buildings lining waterways.

Buildings lining parks.

The legacy masterplan emphasising
the importance of the relationship
between buildings and waterways,
buildings and parks and buildings
and routes.

Buildings lining roads.

Buildings lining waterways, parks and roads.

collection of historical structures within the valley are the group of eighteenth-century mill buildings that lie immediately to the south of the Olympic site.

And so in a way the history of the valley has always been a working history, its plan a response to the practical needs of the wider city. Ironically, however, the more its roads and buildings were configured to fulfil this strategic role, the more weak and fragmented became its local movement infrastructure. So while there are a series of trunk roads which cross the site from east to west, there was, prior to the Games, only one local road which followed a similar route from one side of the valley to the other. One thing the Olympic plan will deliver therefore is a more complex and comprehensive network of connections across the valley – including a series of new bridges – which in turn provide the framework for the legacy development planned to follow the Games.

A similar opening-up has also been possible in the opposite direction. As a tributary of the Thames, the River Lea has always offered the tantalising prospect of a continuous north-south footpath and cycle path linking the centre of the city directly to its rural hinterland. Up till now, the industrial use of the site has prevented this. Because of the Games, this route will now be created, the first of its kind in London and perhaps the only one which will ever be feasible.

One surprising asset of the site, even before the Games were planned, was the quality of its public transport infrastructure: three underground lines, two main line railways, and, in the last two years, an extension of the Docklands Light Railway and the potential for a Eurostar station at Stratford International. The high speed international station and future Crossrail station at Stratford are important in transport terms, but they were also significant because they provided the focus for a major new urban development – Stratford City – the construction of which was substantially progressed prior to the Games. During the Games, Stratford City also provided the location for the Olympic village, home for fifteen thousand athletes, and was designed to revert to residential use after 2012.

So the site of the Olympics is not isolated in some suburban no man's land, but locked firmly into a secure urban context. In fact, Stratford City is one of a series of major development projects in London that reflect a gradual move in the focus of the city towards the east. What precipitated this shift was the decline and subsequent redevelopment of the city's docks, and its most obvious product is the new business district of Canary Wharf. In the past the area of the Lea Valley was perceived as being on the edge of the city, on the divide between the urban and the suburban. Now it is being absorbed into the body of the city itself.

The Olympic Park operated across two, discrete, topographical levels, a lower level set by the waterways that meander through the site, and an upper level defined by the platform of the public concourse on which each of the individual venues are being constructed. The scale and configuration of the concourse was developed principally in response to the estimate of the numbers of people – up to one hundred and forty thousand at any one time – expected to visit the site during the Games. Once the Games were over, the extent of the concourse was to be substantially reduced and areas of paving replaced with grass and trees. In this way, a landscape designed initially to accommodate huge numbers of people at a global event will be able to evolve into one that is tailored to the needs of the local community who will live and work around it. Of the sporting venues, just four have been retained – the main stadium, the aquatics centre, the handball arena and the velodrome – and while each of these buildings maintain their relationship with the park, they also become part of the city that envelops them.

The Legacy masterplan is built on the principle that each of the new, predominantly residential, neighbourhoods that surround the Olympic Park should be designed to look out as well as in, to form explicit connections with the adjacent areas of London of which they form a part. This is important not only for the people who live in the new development, but also for those who live around it. It would be wrong to treat the legacy project as a separate precinct and fail to consider its wider setting. And this

Mews houses.

Terraced houses.

Duplex houses.

Apartment terrace.

Atrium block.

Urban block.

setting is itself undergoing regeneration. In parallel with the development of the Olympic Legacy masterplan, a series of discrete 'fringe' masterplans have been prepared to explore how each of these adjacent areas might be improved and restructured to ensure that they obtain the maximum long-term benefit from the legacy development.

This process of reconnection is not an easy one. When the Games were over, more than a year was required to strip out all the temporary structures, and get all the retained venues fully operational again, and about the same time to remove all the redundant elements from the park and take away the temporary infrastructure provided to service the concourse. It was not until the summer of 2013 that the public were able to return to limited parts of the Olympic Park in advance of its full re-opening in 2014, and even then the park was isolated by the empty areas of land awaiting the legacy development. This is in part an urban design problem: the creation of attractive and secure routes and connections into and across the Olympic Park forms an essential aspect of the post-games transformation project. But it is also in large part a management problem: what, in the short term, will be the best way to draw people into the site and encourage them to use it?

This highlights the important role played by the unexpected and the temporary in shaping the city. The likely colonisation of future legacy development sites by a programme of temporary uses could define aspects of the legacy neighbourhoods' permanent physical, social and economic character, long before new buildings have been designed or constructed. Although interim uses are sometimes seen as a stop-gap to be superseded by the 'vision' the masterplan will bring, real cities are not generally composed of constructed visions. In this instance interim uses might instead prove an essential stage in the process of making the Olympic Park part of London.

2003

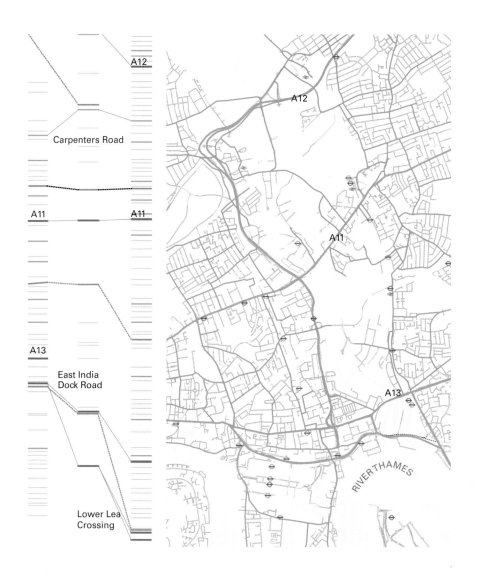

A12

Carpenters Road

A11   A11

A13

East India
Dock Road

Lower Lea
Crossing

A12

A11

A13

RIVER THAMES

OBSERVATION   **Crossing the Lea Valley**

2024

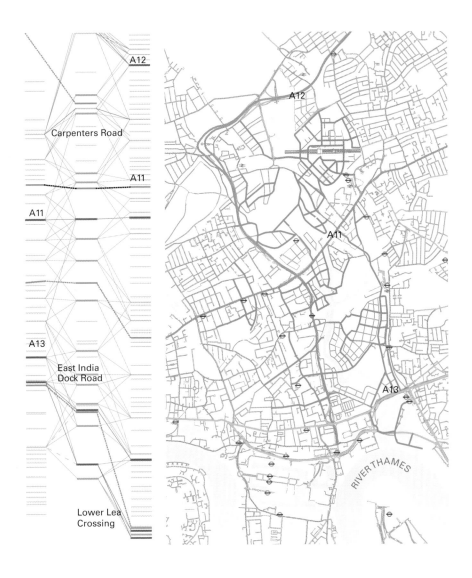

A12

Carpenters Road

A11

A11

A13

East India
Dock Road

Lower Lea
Crossing

A12

A11

A13

RIVER THAMES

Because of its topography, and its complex overlay of industry, transport and utilities, the site of the London Olympic Park was immensely difficult to assimilate and understand. Drawings therefore provided an important means of explaining – to all those involved – the situation we were inheriting.

The two drawings illustrated here were produced to expose the difference between the frequency and variety of existing east–west vehicular and pedestrian routes in the established urban areas on either side of the Lea Valley, and the relative paucity of those present in the valley itself. What this analysis highlighted was the scale of the transformation – and in particular the number of new bridges that would be required – if the Lea Valley were to be provided with the same degree of urban permeability as the more mature – but by no means perfect – pieces of city on either side. The first drawing shows that inherited condition. The second shows the anticipated impact of the Legacy masterplan.

Looking south across the Olympic
site towards Canary Wharf.

Index

Acknowledgements

This book is the result of a wide collaborative effort across the practice.

In addition to the authors of the individual essays many members of the practice, past and present, have contributed to the making of the book and to the thinking that underlies it, including: Paul Appleton, Joanna Bacon, Chris Bearman, Peter Bishop, Jonathan Broughton, Alfredo Caraballo, Artur Carulla, Paul Eaton, Simon Fraser, Simon Gathercole, Helen Hayes, Hendrik Heyns, Raoul Kunz, Miles Leigh, Timothy Makower, Robert Maxwell, Glen Millar, Amanda Moore, Graham Morrison, Ashley Munday, Robert Nisbet, Peter Ohnrich, Lawrie Robertson, Antony Rifkin, Antje Saunders, Christopher Schulte, Emad Sleiby, Jason Syrett, Eddie Taylor, Karin Templin, Steve Walker and Alastair Warburton.

Romy Berlin has been central to the process of developing and designing the book and without her it could not have been realised. Sarah Richards has helped organise the material and source images, while Grainne Crooks was responsible for inputting most of the text and its iterations.

We are also grateful to Mark Swenarton, James Stirling Professor of Architecture at Liverpool University, who read and commented on the manuscript at an early stage, and to Duncan McCorquodale of Artifice who has guided this volume to completion.

The design of large scale masterplanning projects almost always involves a collaboration between many parties: clients, other consultants, local planners. A list of the clients for the projects included in the book is shown below. We also wish to acknowledge in particular the contribution made to the projects by the following:

AECOM; Christopher Bradley-Hole; Eleanor Fawcett; Kathryn Firth; FOA; Jerome Frost; Angus Gavin; Jonathan Joseph; Rachid Karam; LDA Hargreaves; MacCreanor Lavington; Roger Madelin; Rick Mather Associates; Sowmya Parthasarathy; David Partridge; Populous; Porphyrios Associates; Townshend Landscape Architects; Witherford Watson Mann.

We also wish to acknowledge the Wouter Mikmak Foundation, the University of Delft and Sun Publishers who enabled the earlier publication of many of the ideas contained within this book in *Cultivating the City: London before and after 2012* (2010).

King's Cross Central, London; Argent.
Silver Hill, Winchester; Thornfield Properties Plc.
Royal Arsenal Woolwich, London; Berkeley Homes.
Highbury Square, London; Highbury Holdings Ltd.
South Bank, London; Southbank Centre.
Heart of the City, Sheffield; CTP St James Ltd.
Friargate, Coventry; Cannon Cannon Kirk.
District//S, Beirut; Estates Development SAL.
Paper Mill, Wolvercote; Oxford University.
BBC, London; BBC/Land Securities/Bovis Lend Lease.
Brent Cross Cricklewood, London; Hammersmith and City.
Msheireb, Heart of Doha; DohaLand.
Wood Wharf, London; Canary Wharf Group plc.
Aldgate Place, London; Barratt London.
St Andrews Bow, London; Barratt London.
Olympic Games and Legacy, London; Olympic Delivery Authority, London Development Agency. London Organising Committee of the Olympic Games.
Olympic Park Legacy Company, Team Populous.
London Legacy Development Corporation.